Living in Two Worlds

Living in Two Worlds

MIKE COPE

Christian Communications
P. O. Box 150
Nashville, TN 37202

Published by Christian Communications
A Division of Gospel Advocate Co.
P. O. Box 150, Nashville, TN 37202

All scripture quotations in this publication are from the Holy Bible, New International Version. Copyright © 1973, 1978, 1984 International Bible Society. Used by permission of Zondervan Bible Publishers.

1st printing, 1987
2nd printing, 1987
3rd printing, 1988

ISBN 0-89225-297-9

To Diane
A Beautiful Balance of Holiness and Ministry

Acknowledgements

The contribution of others to this book has been great. I want to extend special thanks to Don Humphrey from the Gospel Advocate for encouraging me to get this material into print and to Billie Silvey for her excellent job of editing the oral material.

A note of gratitude should go to Tom Eddins for his valuable suggestions after reading the manuscript. And I certainly appreciate Harold Hazelip, a professor, wordsmith, and preacher par excellence, for penning the foreword.

Mike Cope

Foreword

Mike Cope is a well-trained, highly talented minister of the Word. These meditations on living in two worlds will provide ample evidence of this.

But, hopefully, these pages will accomplish much more in those of us who read them. All of us struggle daily with the tension between living "separate" from the world and serving in the world.

This struggle has historically produced the call to the monastery at one extreme and the announcement of secular Christianity at the other. On the one hand, Simon the Stylite chose to live atop a 72 foot pole for 30 years to avoid contact with a sinful world. The opposite extreme, a call for total involvement in the world, reached a peak in the "death of God" debate of the 1960s.

Mike calls for a Biblical balance between these two demands of the Christian life—holiness and ministry. He spends the first eight chapters of this book in a call for the Christian lifestyle. The old seductions—success, power, sexual freedom, money—are dealt with in fresh and practical ways.

In the last five chapters, his emphasis is on service, involvement with others. He warns that God may grind us in order to use us effectively to infiltrate the world.

He calls for friendship evangelism, challenges us to address the message specifically to the hearer, and depicts the forgiven life as itself an attraction to Christ.

You and I are looking for meaning for our lives. This book comes as a practical guide toward this goal. It is written in personal, conversational style to each of our hearts. It speaks to the challenges of today's world. I hope you will enjoy reading it as much as I did.

Harold Hazelip

Contents

Chapter 1

The Third Race

The tension between a Christian and his society is highlighted in the story Tony Campolo relates of a child who entered his house, not knowing the preacher was visiting. Seeing his mom, the boy came running in holding a rat by the tail. With obvious excitement he choked out: "Look, Mom! Look at this rat I caught out behind the barn! I smashed its head in with a baseball bat! I threw rocks at it! I stomped on it! I spit on it and I, I, I . . . ."

Then he looked up and saw the minister. Swallowing hard he said, "And, and, and then the dear Lord called it home!"

This tension became obvious to me as I sat with some diving friends in a small cafe by the Atlantic Ocean one morning. We were waiting for breakfast since the weather had spoiled our planned excursion. Soon another group of scuba divers who knew my friends but not me joined us. One of them began describing the waitress in graphic (and disgusting) language. My buddies were dying inwardly—if only he knew I was a preacher!

Finally he paused long enough to ask, "What do you do?"

I calmly replied, "I preach for the Pine Valley Church."

He laughed hysterically and asked again, "Really, what do you do?"

I smiled and said, "I told you. I preach for the Pine Valley Church."

This time his smile was nervous as he glanced at one of my friends, who nodded in agreement. Quickly he straightened up, changed tones, and said, "My brother took a theology class at Duke." I was somewhat underwhelmed!

It is an awkward position we Christians are in. We participate in two worlds. We are already in a new dimension, having been raised with Christ. But we have not yet been fully redeemed from the old nature. We already have participated in new life, but we have not yet experienced the final resurrection.

What is the relationship between those who have been born again and the world where they were first born? Is any synthesis possible between Christ and culture?

Toward a Synthesis

In 1951, H. Richard Niebuhr wrote *Christ and Culture*, in which he outlined three possible relationships between Christ and society: 1) Christ and culture in antithesis, 2) Christ and culture completely intertwined, and 3) Christ and culture different but needing to be united in some way.

Niebuhr believed that we must seek the third route—that we must try to infiltrate our culture with the gospel of Christ.

The relationship between Christ and culture is not a new issue. Christians at the end of the second century struggled with it. The anonymous writer of "The Epistle of Diognetus" said:

Yet while living in Greek and barbarian cities according as each obtained his lot and following the local customs both in clothing and in food and in the rest of life, Christians show forth a wonderful and confessedly strange character of the constitution of their own citizenship. They dwell in their own fatherlands but as if sojourners in them. They share all things as citizens and suffer all things as strangers. Every foreign country is their fatherland and every fatherland is their foreign country. They marry as all men. They bear children, but they don't expose their offspring. They offer free hospitality but guard their purity. Their lot is cast in the flesh but they do not live after the flesh. They pass their time upon the earth but they have their citizenship in heaven. They obey the appointed laws and they surpass the laws in their own lives.

Shortly after that was written, some Christians began calling themselves the Third Race. They weren't Jews, and they weren't exactly Gentiles. They struggled with the issue of relating to the world while holding citizenship in heaven.

The issue faced by those early Christians confronts us today. How do we relate to our world? Two key words from scripture help us answer that question.

The First Word: Holiness

John Bunyan wrote, "Apollyon, beware what you do, for I am in the King's highway—the way of holiness and, therefore, take heed to yourself." All of us are pilgrims on this King's highway of holiness.

Throughout the New Testament we read of saints. To some this conjures up images of superspiritual people— people who have hit all the good things in life, who have overcome all sins, who are ahead of everyone else. The Roman Catholic Church has influenced such thinking by canonizing certain individuals and calling them saints.

In the New Testament, however, saints are the rank and file members of the church—not the spiritually elite, but all who have been called into Jesus Christ. We are a holy people, set aside by God for a special purpose (Titus 2:14). (For the Old Testament roots of this thought, see Deuteronomy 7:6; 14:2; and 26:18.)

God set us apart in baptism. He's declared us to be holy because of the atonement of Christ. Now we are called upon to live that way (1 Peter 1:15; James 1:27; 4:4). But how?

John (1 John 2:15-17) and Paul (2 Corinthians 6:14-7:1) emphasized the separation that should characterize Christians. Don't partake of the unholiness of the world, they warned us. Don't indulge in its values or mindset. Be special. Don't love the world.

We should purify ourselves from everything that contaminates body and spirit, perfecting holiness out of reverence for God. If we don't, the uniqueness that should permeate our lives will be absent.

The Second Word: Ministry

While our citizenship is in heaven, we are now residents of this earth. We're pilgrims or aliens, but while we're here, we must live with and serve the people around us.

Consider the ministry of Jesus. He was here to serve (Mark 10:45), to help sinners (Mark 2:17), and he called on us to do the same thing. Our place is not in a monastery. We are to be out in the world, as Paul was, serving as ministers (1 Corinthians 9:19-23).

Both holiness and ministry are important. To be holy, our value system and actions must be different from those of the world. To minister we must be out in the world letting the influence of Christ be felt.

The Balancing Act

What happens if we have holiness but no ministry, or ministry but no holiness? What happens if we have both? Three models will help us answer those questions.

Rejectionist

The first model is the unbalanced rejectionist. He has holiness and separation—to the point of radicalism—but he lacks ministry; he doesn't identify with the world.

Before the time of Jesus, some like-minded Jewish separatists had gathered near the Dead Sea to protect their purity. Their famous scrolls (the Dead Sea Scrolls) have pointed toward their rejectionist outlook. The following is found in their "Scroll of the Rule": "And this is the rule for the members of the Community for those who volunteer to be converted from all evil and to cling to all [the Teacher's] commands according to his will; to

Immersionist

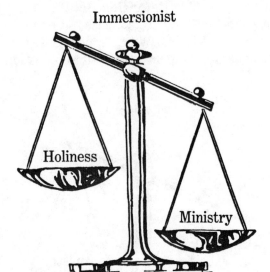

separate themselves from the congregation of perverse men, to become a Community in the Law."

How many of us follow this example to a lesser degree? We like to be sheltered by having people around us who think as we do. We secretly desire to do business only with Christians, to be educated only with Christians, and to live only around Christians.

If that is our viewpoint, we are unbalanced rejectionists. We are hiding our candle under a bushel. We may be proud of our light, but nobody sees it.

The second model is the unbalanced immersionist. He is big on ministry and intense identification. He is in the world. He listens to the music of the world uncritically and sees every movie, but he becomes very light on holiness.

Germany in the 1920s and '30s was an educated culture. But after Hitler came to office in 1933, it wasn't long until doctors, lawyers, ministers, theologians, and psychiatrists were working for the Nazis. It was a time that called for Christians to be radically different. You can't always flow with the cultural tide.

This second imbalance isn't light hidden under a bushel. It isn't light at all. There is only darkness. Unbalanced immersionists are socially integrated, but they're not spiritually distinct.

The third model is a balance of both holiness and ministry. It is the synthesis of Christ and culture. It's not Christ against culture; that's too radical. Nor is it Christ intertwined with culture, because often he's different. It's the model that says that on the one hand I must be holy. God calls me to distinctive living. But on the other hand, I must also have a ministry. The church must be in the world without having too much of the world in the church.

Balanced View

Jesus spoke to this issue as he was about to leave his disciples (John 17:13ff). In his high priestly prayer he said, "Sanctify them, Father. Set them apart. Let them know they are not of the world. Yet, Father, I'm sending them into the world. They're ministers. They are to exercise a leavening influence in the world. They are salt and light. They are the aroma of good news" (paraphrased).

Our goal is to combine holiness and ministry—to be a light not hidden under a bushel, to be socially integrated yet spiritually distinct. If either concept is missing from your life, something is wrong with your view of Christ and culture.

Thought Questions for Chapter 1

1. In which area do you believe most Christians are more deficient: holiness or ministry?
2. Read the following newspaper article (Jan. 29, 1983) and consider ways we could make the same mistakes: "A Pentecostal preacher has been jailed for isolating his wife and seven children at their rural home to keep them from being 'contaminated by the world.' The Rev. Juan Eliceo Garcia was charged with depriving his 32-year-old wife, Santa Benita Justiniano, and the children of their liberty over a period of five years."
3. Is it harder to avoid the behavior or the value system of the world?
4. Do some study on the word "saint" (which is related in the language of the New Testament to holiness). To whom does the word properly apply?

Chapter 2

America's Battle Cry: Success!

A 25th high school reunion is somewhat like judgment day—a time of reckoning what we've done in this body, whether good or bad, of judging one another's success. Who drove up in the BMW? Who drove up in the battered Plymouth? Who managed to marry above himself? Who did about what we expected? Who has the most prestigious job? Who lives on the best side of town? On and on we go in this reckoning.

Some come to these reunions hardly able to wait for somebody to ask that all-important question: What are you doing? They're dying to spurt it out—this is what I'm doing! I'm so important! Others, on the other hand, go begging the Lord that no one will ask. It all depends on their perspective of success.

Success is our national battle cry. We eat it, breathe it, caress it, baby it, and even worse, judge ourselves by it. If I think I've lived up to society's standards for success, I'm a success. My ego is in good shape. I feel good about myself, so I treat you well. But if I don't think society sees me as a success, I see myself as a failure.

In America we pay homage to the trinity of wealth, power, and prestige. We bow down before them. If we cannot find them in life, we think we've missed our calling

As God's people, have we managed to stay separate from society's view of success, or have we bought into that view?

Leonard Allen has written a piercing article that includes these words:

> There's a growing tendency to adopt the narcissistic language of psychological self-help theories and masquerade it as gospel preaching. And, in the process, turn the gospel into a do-it-yourself formula for happy homes, robust sex, easy money and quick inner peace. There's a trend toward allowing the "me" generation to dictate the terms in which we proclaim the gospel of the dying and rising Christ. In general, there's the powerful but subtle pressure to intertwine Christian values with middle class values, Christian destiny with American destiny, Christian sacrifice with the sacrifices of Republican economics, Christian success with Zig Ziglar's success. Only serious theological reflection, only fresh grappling with the Biblical text in light of our past and present, can provide the resources for coping with the ferment and addressing the dangers.

If we judge ourselves on the basis of success, we need to carve our view of success from the parable of the rich man and Lazarus (Luke 16). Let's consider two views of success from the parable. The first is the high school reunion view (verses 19-21).

If you showed up at a reunion at Jerusalem High, how would you view the rich man? Based on the national trinity of wealth, power, and prestige, he's done well. The text says "he lives in luxury everyday." He's got a mansion in the best part of town. He's got purple robes and silk undies. As he strolls up from his hand-carved, gold-trimmed chariot, people look at him and say,

"There's a man who's made it in life!" When minutes are sent out later, they'll probably mention him first.

In contrast, we're embarrassed that somebody sent Lazarus an invitation. We try to forget he graduated from the same high school. He's covered with open sores. He stinks. We can hardly stand it as he walks in the door. He's malnourished. He sits at the rich man's gate and waits for crumbs from his table.

But there's another view that comes from the parable—the eternal view. Lazarus died, and the angels carried him to Abraham's side. The rich man also died and was buried. And in Hades he looked up and saw Lazarus and wanted just a drop of water to cool his scorching tongue.

We've had a reversal of roles between the high school reunion and the eternal view of success. We're an eternal people if we're God's people. Let's consider three insights into success from the eternal view of this parable:

1. Success has more to do with how you treat people than with how they treat you. The people at the Jerusalem reunion are glad the rich man came. They probably bow down to him. James noted how we have a tendency to kowtow to people of prestige and wealth (James 2). Probably the people who know the rich man, whether they like him or not, want to be on his good side. They want him at their parties because it says something about them. What a wonderful portfolio could be made with the rich man's name as a reference!

By this view of success, Jesus did his best job, hit the pinnacle of his ministry, in the triumphal entry into Jerusalem (Luke 19). People ripped off their coats and cut down palm branches to put over the yellow brick road into the city.

But Luke told us that real success is found not on the road to Jerusalem, but on the cross just outside the city gates. Luke showed us that success is not how people treat you, but how you treat others. Jesus had been saying, "I've come for you. I've come to die." It was because he loved us so much that he gave himself on the old rugged cross.

If Jesus walked into a high school reunion, I think these are the kinds of questions he'd be asking: How have you been treating your wife lately? How much time have you been spending with your kids? What concern do you have for those with inadequate housing and nutrition?

2. *Success has more to do with God's view of you than with other peoples' views of you.* Again, if we start with the rich man at the high school reunion, he's doing quite well. He's probably in every "Who's Who" published— "Who's Who in Jerusalem," "Who's Who in Palestine," even the big volume called "Who's Who in the Roman Empire." If success is how people view you, he has it made.

Sociologists tell us that we feel successful if the most successful people in our lives deem us successful. What makes children feel successful? When Mom and Dad tell them they're of worth. That's why I hate to hear parents jokingly refer to their kids as worms or messes. Once in a while they may know by the tone of voice that their parents are kidding, but when it's constant, they start to think of themselves that way.

How do teenagers typically come to their self-esteem? It isn't from parents but from peers—the people around them at school or church, their immediate, significant others. Teenagers want to be perceived as successful, especially by the opposite sex.

A girl wants to be asked out by the most popular boy in

school, not necessarily because she wants to go out witn *him*, but because she wants everybody to know she's going out with him. Her self-esteem depends on how others view her. A boy fantasizes about accomplishing great athletic feats to prove himself to that special someone in the stands. He wants to see himself as successful through the lenses of other people's glasses.

How do adults come to their view of success? No longer is it through parents or immediate peers. Rather, it's from everybody in general but nobody in particular. We want people in the world to think we're somebody. We want to be perceived as successful. And if we think this way, we're setting ourselves up for a tremendous midlife crisis, because people won't always have that view of us.

We may grow up to be like Willy Loman in "The Death of a Salesman"—discarded by society, no longer wanted as a salesman, not wanted for anything. He felt the only way out was death.

If our view of success is to be correct, we can't seek success through other people's eyes. We need the significant other person in our lives to be God Almighty (Hebrews 13:20-21) and to see success as faithfulness to the ministry he's given us.

3. Success has to do more with internal qualities than with external circumstances. It can't be right that one boy is more valuable than another because of where he bought his jeans. It can't be right for millions of American women to feel like complete zeros because they can't measure up to the statistics of a 20-year-old strutting on a ramp in Atlantic City. It can't be right to deify a young man because of an athletic ability with which he was born. We cannot, as God's people, buy into the concept of success through external circumstances.

Erma Bombeck once filled her humorous pen with serious ink and wrote the following words:

> On the first Saturday of last month a 22-year-old U.S. tennis player hoisted a silver bowl over his head at center court at Wimbledon. On the day before five blind mountain climbers, one man with an artificial leg, an epileptic and two deaf adventurers stood atop the snow-capped summit of Mt. Ranier. It was a noisy victory for the tennis player who shared it with 14,000 fans, some of whom had slept on the sidewalks outside the club for six nights waiting for tickets. It was a quiet victory for the climbers who led their own cheering. There was a lot of rhetoric exchanged at Wimbledon regarding bad calls. At Mt. Ranier they learned to live with life's bad calls a long time ago . . . . In our search for heroes and heroines we often lose our perspective . . . . Hero is a term that should be awarded to those who, given a set of circumstances, react with courage, dignity, decency and compassion—people who make us feel better by having seen or touched them. I think the crowds went to the wrong summit and cheered the wrong champion.

What is your view of success? Review the parable from God's perspective. Concentrate on treating others as Jesus would. Emphasize internals, not externals. Make God your significant other person so that your goal becomes to please him alone.

Thought Questions for Chapter 2

1. God's reign in the world has been called "the upside down kingdom." In what sense would this be true?
2. At the end of Tom Peters' 1985 best-seller, *A Passion for Excellence,* he wrote:

"We are frequently asked if it is possible to 'have it all'—a full and satisfying personal life and a full and satisfying, hard-working, professional one. Our answer is: No. The price of excellence is time, energy, attention and focus, at the very same time that energy, attention and focus could have gone toward your daughter's soccer game. Excellence is a high-cost item."

Reflect on the implications of this for defining Christian excellence.

3. In what ways might we unintentionally communicate a worldly model of success to our children?
4. By what criteria does God determine the success of a person?

Chapter 3

The Gospel According to Rambo

"Beads of sweat glisten. Pectoral muscles ripple. Veins bulge in steamy close-up. They call him a pure fighting machine—this glum-faced superhero with a Charles Atlas body. He's been sent on a mission to Viet Nam—a land that just a few years ago the nation was trying to forget. Improbably, or maybe all too probably, he has become America's newest pop hero. His name— Rambo."

So reads *Time* magazine concerning Rambomania. Rambo is Sylvester Stallone's 1985 superhero. Many identify with him. He reflects, not a way to change culture, but what culture already is. It's the innate desire to control other people, to be powerful, to manipulate. It's J. R. Ewing with a machine gun.

Time also talked about Rambomania in the toy stores. You can buy a $150 replica of his high-powered bow and arrow. You can buy a Rambo knife, a Rambo automatic squirt gun, and Rambo vitamins. New Yorkers who want a raise from the boss can send a Rambo-gram.

We've even got a Rambo in the White House at the time of this writing. People are awed by a president who recovers so well from cancer and surgery. He comes back from being shot to serve two terms. He lifts weights every day and publishes a book about it.

This attitude influences our culture's talk about nuclear war. We complain that the Russians could kill everyone seven times while we could only do it four or five times. The emphasis is on power and control.

The German philosopher Friedrich Nietzsche said that the will to power is an innate desire. It's the desire to control other people. Nietzsche believed that God was dead—if he ever existed—and that man had to be in control. What Nietzsche's philosophy demonstrates is that if your greatest desire is to be powerful, you have to get rid of God, because God is bigger than you are.

These desires for Rambo-like power go back to the earliest days when the serpent said to Adam and Eve, "Would you like to be like God? Would you like to be powerful? Would you like to control? Would you like to see like God? To know like God? Then eat some of the fruit he's forbidden. He just doesn't want you to have the power he does." They wanted power as much as we do, so they ate the fruit.

Games People Play

Politicians play power games because they have positions of power. Sennacherib, Nebuchadnezzar, Alexander, Nero, and Hitler are names that drip with the sweat of power. They wanted more and more. Herod the Great even killed his sons rather than let them vie for his power. Solomon must also be added to the list. Samuel had warned the people of Israel, "You don't need a king, because he'll soak you for all you're worth. He'll crave power." And Solomon did. He enslaved and overtaxed his people.

Not all politicans are like this. Some want to change society for good. But others got where they are because they like power. They drink it up.

29

An American Life—One Man's Way to Watergate is Jeb Stuart MacGruder's story of his involvement in Watergate. MacGruder was a young, articulate, well-educated Californian who was called to take on a responsible position within the administration of President Richard Nixon. MacGruder details how he forgot his ethics, violated his morality, and put behind him all he'd learned about right and wrong. Why? "I was close to the seat of power," he explained.

Near the end of his autobiography, MacGruder wrote, "For fifteen years I fought to reach the pinnacle of our society. I got very close to the top and I found that it wasn't all it was supposed to be. To get there and to stay there you have to pay a price too high in your private life. Obviously, in my case, ambitions led to disaster." MacGruder got caught. Many others don't.

Power games occur in dating. One example is withholding love. It's the Principle of Least Interest. Never make an emotional commitment, never tell your date that you enjoy the relationship, and you can exercise control. For example, a couple has been dating for a year, but he's never told her he's glad they're dating. He never says anything about their relationship. He just keeps asking her out, and she's not sure why. He's emotionally aloof because if he's aloof, he's in control. Although he thinks he's smart, he's probably just watched too many James Bond movies where he learned to be emotionally detached while romantically involved.

Another game in dating is when you don't forgive. You may learn something of a person's past, or that person may offend you. So you say, "That's all right. Let's go on." But you never forgive the person, and your knowledge of his or her past becomes your trump card. Whenever there's friction in the relationship, you bring it up. It's a power game that says, "I have control over you. You remember what happened back there? I'm the offended party. So let me have my way now."

These games are played in marriages, too. Husbands withhold love. Some never tell their wives they love them. They just come home to eat at the end of the day. The wife is left wondering, *Am I still attractive to him? Is our marriage going anywhere?* He's playing a power game.

A husband can also play power games by misusing his leadership and handing down unilateral decisions. "This is what we're going to do." "This is what I decided for the children." "We're moving to Philadelphia tomorrow." He knows the Bible passages about being the head of the family, but not the ones about loving his wife.

Another power game is played when husbands compliment other women. "Doesn't Alice always have her house in order?" But his wife knows he means, "Why do I have to live in a pig sty?" Or he says, "Have you ever noticed how Suzie keeps fit?" The real message is, "Why don't you carve some fat off your hips?" She gets these subtle messages. When he tells her something about these other women, he's got power over her. She's left worried and wondering where she stands.

Wives play power games, too. Those who have bought into the radical element of the women's movement have been encouraged to face bossy husbands by being bossy wives. It's a power game.

Some withhold sex as a way of manipulating a husband. It's like saying, "If Roger is a good little boy, he can have sex tonight." Others play power games by pouting and crying, "You don't know how miserable I am." Sometimes it's genuine, but sometimes it's a means of control. It's the Delilah syndrome. "Oh, Samson, you don't love me. If you really loved me, you'd tell me the source of your power."

Children also play power games. They threaten Mom and Dad with, "If you don't let me have my way, I'll pack up and leave" or, "I'm going to do something horrible that you'll always regret." And then there's, "I'm going to embarrass you publicly, and you'll never be able to show your face again."

Employers play power games. They do it by causing their employees to worry about losing their jobs. They never express appreciation. A boss may say, "I've just got to cut back on the staff one of these days."

Of course, employees play power games, too. They may say, "If you try to make me do anything I don't want to do, I'll file a grievance with the union." While there are legitimate places for unions, Christians shouldn't use them as a way to manipulate others.

Religious legalists play power games. They can't stand the thought of being saved by someone else—even God. That represents a loss of control. "I want to have power. I want to save myself," is their attitude. Religious legalists preach on grace, but not Paul's meaning of the word. A legalist envisions God's taking up the last few items he couldn't quite make. Grace is not God's taking up the slack; it's God's taking over.

In friendship some play power games as well. In his book *The Friendship Factor*, Alan Loy McGinnis talked about three kinds of manipulators in friendships. First, there are the "take charge" manipulators. They always have to call the shots. You always go to *their* restaurants. You always do what *they* want to do. They aren't happy unless they're in the driver's seat.

Second, there are the "poor me" manipulators. "Poor me. Things are so bad. You don't know how bad they are.

The things last week have been solved, but I've got worse things this week." I counseled a lady like that one time. Nothing could make her happier than a tragedy that gave her an excuse to "poor me" you.

Third is the "need to be needed" type. This person says, "I'm always available. You can always tell me." It may be a mother who wants her daughter to have marital problems and come running with "Oh, Mom, I've got problems." Such a mother loves to be needed.

Jesus and Power

If anyone could have played power games, it was Jesus. He was "in very nature God" (Philippians 2:6). In his preincarnate state, he was equal with God. He was God himself, God the Son. That's an impressive portfolio for power. He was in the nature of God, yet he didn't consider equality with God something to be grasped. He came to a culture that thrived on power, and he chose powerlessness. He chose the way of love rather than the way of Rambo. He chose love over power. He "made himself nothing" (Philippians 2:7).

Jesus didn't come as a Superbaby or Superboy who dazzled his friends with magic. Some people wish he did. There are some early "gospels," not written by the inspiration of God, composed in the second and third centuries. One says that Jesus killed some of his friends when they made him mad. Another says he was playing with a little boy who fell off a roof, and Jesus went down and raised him from the dead. A third tells of his making a little clay bird and bringing it to life.

These stories are not in harmony with the biblical account. The Bible says that Jesus was born as a vulnerable infant to parents who were known to few people in a tiny town in an insignificant province: "Taking the very nature of a servant, being made in human likeness" (Philippians 2:7).

During his manhood, people tried to force him to play power games. In Luke 4, Satan said, "Climb to the top of the temple, jump off, and let tens of thousands of angels come to your rescue." That was a call to play power games. Jesus wanted people to repent, leave everything, and follow him. Those were high demands for discipleship, and many would turn him down. Satan said, "If you jump off the temple, people will flock to you." But Jesus wouldn't play his game.

On another occasion, 5,000 men gathered in the desert and tried to make him king by force. They needed a military general to lead them into Jerusalem to oust the Romans. Jesus wouldn't play that game either.

In the Garden of Gethsemane, Peter tried to play the game. When Judas came with the authorities, Peter whipped out his sword and cut off Malchus's ear. But Jesus said, "Peter, I'm not playing that game."

Remember the power games of James and John? They came to Jesus and said, "Master, can we have the places of power when you come into your kingdom?"

Jesus replied, "Let me talk to you about suffering."

Jesus steadfastly refused to play power games. He took the nature of a servant. He refused to manipulate people. He chose love over power.

"And being found in appearance as a man, he humbled himself and became obedient to death—even death on a cross!" (Philippians 2:8). Jesus was not a Rambo storming the gates of Jerusalem with his automatic weapon. He was a broken man, crucified shamefully on a Roman cross outside the city gates. He chose love, even in the form of suffering, over power games.

34

Learning the Lesson of Jesus

How does all this apply to us? First, we must rely on our weakness before God. Paul pointed out that false teachers say you must have power before God. Paul laid out his portfolio and said, "You want to play power games? Here are my credentials: I was circumcised on the eighth day and I belong to the tribe of Benjamin. A Hebrew of Hebrews. As regards the law, a Pharisee. As for zeal, persecuting the church. As for legalistic righteousness, faultless" (Philippians 3).

"But I'm not going to rely on some power structure before God," he continued. "I'm going to rely on my own weakness, so I can know Christ and the power of his resurrection."

In his second letter to the church at Corinth, Paul put it another way: "To keep me from being conceited because of the surpassing great revelations, there was given me a thorn in my flesh—a messenger of Satan—to torment me. Three times I pleaded with the Lord to take it from me. But he said to me, 'My grace is sufficient for you. For my power is made perfect in weakness.' Therefore, I will boast all the more gladly about my weakness so that Christ's power may rest on me."

That's not power; it's weakness. It's the way of the cross. Rely on your weakness. God will use you more in weakness when you count on his grace than when you're trying to stand on your own rights.

Second, rely on your meekness. Meekness is not a big word in the Rambo vocabulary. It sounds "wimpy." But meekness means you have your strength under control. There's still power, but it submits to love. Instead of living with love for power, we live, as Huey Lewis sings, by "the power of love." They are entirely different things.

Some Christians in Philippi were apparently playing power games. They were jockeying for position. Paul said, "Your attitude should be the same as that of Christ Jesus." He didn't talk about Jesus just out of biographical interest. He wanted the Christians there to live that way. Instead of struggling for power in the Philippian church, they were to give in to the power of love.

If we're going to live with a connection between Christ and culture, we must oppose power plays. We must oppose efforts to use people, control them, manipulate them. We must live by the power that sent Jesus to the cross.

Power games will ruin the people you play them with, and they'll ruin you, too. If you've been manipulating people and controlling them against their will, go back to the groundwork of Philippians 2 and start living a life of service.

Thought Questions for Chapter 3

1. The chapter names several power games that are commonly played. What other examples could you give?
2. Read John 13:1-17. What implications should this lesson of action have on our view of power and love?
3. See Mark 10:42-45 and 1 Peter 5:1-4. What warnings did Jesus and Peter give to church leaders who might seek positions of power?
4. Is it possible to love someone "with no strings attached"?

Chapter 4

Living in a Sex-Saturated Society

Imagine that suddenly some kind of volcanic eruption buried the United States. Even the Rockies were encased. About two centuries from now, archaeologists dig down to where our civilization was. What would they find? What would they say about us? What kind of values would they ascribe to us in their twenty-second-century books?

They might say that we were enamored with success, that we were power hungry, that we were materialistic. And what if they found some magazines that weren't completely ruined by lava or some tapes of television advertising or newspaper ads? Wouldn't they find that the key to selling was sex? They'd see sex used to sell perfume, blue jeans, aftershave lotion, ballpoint pens, fertilizer—anything you can think of.

Those researchers might also come across some of our television programming and discover that the average American watches twelve hundred hours of television a year, compared with just five hours spent reading books. They might find the Michigan State study that showed that soap operas average two sexual acts per program— 94 per cent between couples who aren't married. They would logically conclude that we were a sex-oriented society.

In his book *Christians in the Wake of the Sexual Revolution*, Randy Alcorn tells of two days he spent watching television:

> Because I don't watch much television, I wanted to get a broad and accurate exposure to current programming. So I bought an issue of *TV Guide* and spent two vacation days flipping from channel to channel, watching many programs I had never seen (and, Lord willing, will never see again).
>
> I saw several unmarried couples sleep together, discovered an X-rated bakery in New York and a gigolo convention in New Jersey, listened to a sex researcher on a popular talk show, and watched one movie in which everyone's clothes disintegrated and another of a brutal rape in a New England village. I saw the usual corruption and adultery on "Dynasty" and "Dallas," a leering game show host making sexual comments to a young woman, and X-rated story lines with B-rated acting on daytime soap operas.

Alcorn was describing what people would find if they unearthed our civilization and watched the programs that come into our homes every evening.

What if they listened to our music? I'm sure they would find the raunchy, sexual lyrics in some rock music nearly as bad as those of some Country-Western music, and that's pretty bad. They might hear songs like this one from Bruce Springsteen:

> Hey, little girl, is your daddy home? Did he go away and leave you all alone? I got a bad desire. I'm on fire! Tell me now, Baby, is he good to you? Can he do to you the things that I do? I can take you higher . . . Only you can cool my desire. I'm on fire!

That doesn't leave a lot to the imagination!

What about the novels we read? If the archaeologists

dug through to the novels on some bookshelves—not the great, classic novels, because few read those, but things like Harlequin romances—and discovered that they were put out to the tune of sixty new romances per month with about 20,000,000 readers per year, they'd get a distinct view of our culture.

What if they came across some of our pornography? They might be shocked if they started flipping through *Playboy*. But then they'd find other publications that make Hugh Hefner look like St. Frances of Assisi. *Boy!* they'd think, *what kind of twisted people were they?*

They might find movies that were popular in the 1980's, like "Casual Sex," pretty well representative of a whole genre of movies.

They might read some of our favorite philosophers. Many in the United States subscribe to the views of Bertrand Russell, who said that entering into marriage without prior sexual involvement is "just as absurd as it would be if a man, intending to buy a horse, were not allowed to view it until he had completed the purchase." Or they'd find psychologists like Albert Ellis, who wrote in his book *Sex Without Guilt:*

> It may be said with little fear of scientific contradiction that literally millions of men and women who engage in adulterous affairs thereby gain considerable adventure and experience, become more competent at sexual pursuits and practices, are able to partake of a high degree of varietism and have substantial amounts of sexual and non-sexual fun that they otherwise would doubtlessly be denied. These, in a world that tends to be as dull and drab for the average man as our own, are no small advantages.

What would the archaeologists of the future think of us in the United States? They might conclude that we spend one-third of our time having sex, one-third planning to have sex, and the other third talking about the sex we've had. They might call us the sex-saturated society.

You can't get away from this sexual insanity. In November 1986, children in Lund, Nevada, calling Santa on a special number advertised over a Salt Lake City television station, got instead a woman describing an illegal sex act on a "Dial-a-Porn" number. The number for Santa Claus in one state was the same number for kinky sexual thrills in another state.

We need to seek sexual sanity. How do we as God's people live in a culture that is so saturated with sex? Let's consider four basic biblical principles:

1. God created us as sexual beings. You wouldn't know this from much of church history, because there's a rather dark cloud hovering over the subject in its annals. You might go to Jerome, who spoke of sex as something evil, or to Origen, one of the early church fathers who taught that sex was inherently wrong. Augustine said sex was part of the original sin of Genesis 3, and that kind of thinking still carries over into many churches today.

The Pope, for example, is very vocal against birth control, thinking that a couple should never have sex without the possibility of conceiving children—never solely for enjoyment—a negative approach to sexuality But it doesn't come from Genesis 1. Genesis 1 doesn't smack of Victorian or any other negative approach to sexuality.

"So God created man in his own image, in the image of God he created him; male and female he created them" (Genesis 1:27). No one should have to apologize for having sexual feelings and thoughts, because God made us as sexual beings. It's programmed into us as part of our humanity. The first thing we have to affirm, then, is that sex is not wrong. The concept of sex comes from God.

He could have made us all one gender. He could have come up with other ways for the race to continue, but he made male and female. So don't apologize for having sexual feelings. It's God who made you either male or female. It's his design that you should be a sexual being.

2. Sex is to be enjoyed in marriage. It's important that young people in the church hear this from the pulpit, because if it's never discussed in a church setting, negative vibrations come into the skull. If you never hear anyone say that sex is a gift of God, given for the sanctity of marriage, then you think it's something we don't talk about in the same context as God. You compartmentalize it. It's something you talk about in other places, but not in a church building.

God has a positive view of sex. It's a gift from him for the committed relationship of marriage. "For this reason a man will leave his father and mother and be united to his wife and they will become one flesh" (Genesis 2:24). That one-flesh union is an intertwining of personalities, involving the emotional and the spiritual as well as the physical.

Was it just for child-bearing? Was it just so Adam and Eve could have Cain and Abel? We don't read about children until later in the book. In Genesis 2 it's just a gift of God given to the marriage relationship. Eve didn't look at it as a wifely duty. It was something for which they both thanked God.

Even in the context of a warning against an adulterous relationship, there is a positive stream of the beauty of sex in the marriage relationship:

Drink water from your own cistern, running water from your own well. Should your springs overflow in the streets, your streams of water in the public squares? Let them be yours alone, never to be shared with strangers. May your

41

fountain be blessed, and may you rejoice in the wife of your youth. A loving doe, a graceful deer—may her breasts satisfy you always, may you ever be captivated by her love. Why be captivated, my son, by an adulteress? Why embrace the bosom of another man's wife? For a man's ways are in full view of the Lord, and he examines all his paths" (Proverbs 5:15-21).

There's a whole book in the Old Testament that sounds just like this—the Song of Solomon. It's there to tell you that sex is good in the context of marriage. In that committed relationship, it is a gift of God. It's not something for the church to condemn or ignore.

In the New Testament, Paul wrote:

The husband should fulfill his marital duty [speaking about the sexual relationship] to his wife, and likewise the wife to her husband. The wife's body does not belong to her alone but also to her husband. In the same way, the husband's body does not belong to him alone but also to his wife. Do not deprive each other except by mutual consent and for a time, so that you may devote yourselves to prayer. Then come together again so that Satan will not tempt you because of your lack of self-control (1 Corinthians 7:3-5).

The intimate relationship isn't a tool for manipulation. It's a gift. The marriage bed is undefiled (Hebrews 13). Loving his people so much, wanting to give them this joy of full intimacy in marriage, God sanctified sex in that relationship.

3. Sexual intimacy outside of marriage is wrong. Don't confuse what's taking place in the United States since the sexual revolution with what we've just read in the Bible. Anything can be abused and made harmful. Water is a healthful thing; we'd die of thirst without it.

But in massive amounts, it can flood an entire community. Fire warms us in the winter, guides us in the night, and cooks our food, but too much of it out of control can destroy a forest. Sexuality is the same. Within its God-given boundaries, it's beautiful. But if we abuse it, it can destroy us.

God's people are called to a holy lifestyle (1 Thessalonians 4:3-8; Ephesians 5:3-7; 1 Corinthians 6:12-20). Two words are used in the New Testament for the violation of this holiness—fornication and adultery. Fornication means intimate sexual relationship outside of marriage. It could be homosexuality, adultery, or premarital sex. Adultery is more specific. It means sex in which one of the partners is married to another person.

Why should we be sexually pure? Let me give you two reasons. First, God says to. That may be the easiest answer. If you've just bought a computer and you ask the people you bought it from, "Why can't I wash the insides with soap and water?" the best answer might be that the manufacturer warns against it. The company made the computer. Its engineers know what's inside and what's harmful to it. Likewise, God made sex, and he set boundaries so we wouldn't abuse it. He knows us. He made us. He knows what will happen if we abuse our sexuality.

Second, sex was intended for a complete commitment. All of us who counsel find people whose lives are messed up because they experimented beyond God's boundaries. They thought sexuality was limited to one situation and wouldn't affect other aspects of their lives. That's wrong. Sex is part of a full union. In marriage it's part of a lot of different unions—of spirits, of commitments, of time together. You can't separate it and say, "We're going to have this sexual relationship and forget about the other

43

relationships." The beauty of marriage is that God's people say, "I'm taking you until death do us part." Sex blossoms on this secure basis. It doesn't depend on emotional highs and lows. It's not a way to get somebody or to appease our own feelings.

C. S. Lewis in his book *The Four Loves* said:

> We use the most unfortunate idiom when we say, of a lustful man prowling the streets, that he "wants a woman." Strictly speaking, a woman is just what he does not want. He wants a pleasure for which a woman happens to be the necessary piece of apparatus. How much he cares about the woman as such may be gauged by his attitude to her five minutes after fruition.

How can we remain sexually pure? First, avoid situations in which your immediate feelings will take over. Psychologist Henry Brandt's son was upset because his father wouldn't let him go out alone on a date in a car. "What's wrong, Dad?" he asked. "Don't you trust me?"

His dad said, "In a car? Alone at night with a girl? I wouldn't trust me. Why should I trust you?"

The point is clear. Don't get in situations in which emotions decide.

Second, don't feed on lustful material. We can't win the battle if we're constantly putting the wrong things into our minds. We can't feed our minds on titillating romances or pornography or movies that stimulate the imagination and expect it not to affect us. Read Philippians 4 again, and feed on things that are good and right and pure.

Third, remember who you are. To me this is critical, because I want to follow in Christ's steps. I want to be able to come to him with no little closets reserved and say, "Lord, you take over." Paul did that. He said, "Don't you know you're not your own? You're bought with a price" (1 Corinthians 6:19-20). The Holy Spirit lives within you. When you're involved with sexual immorality, you're not the only one who's desecrated, because the Spirit is dwelling in the temple of your body.

Finally, turn the battle over to God. Count on his full armor (Ephesians 6:10-17).

4. Sexual sins can be forgiven. We haven't preached on this enough. The Bible doesn't say that sexual sins are sins unto death. When Jesus saw someone caught up in sexual sins, he saw them primarily as candidates for forgiveness. The woman caught in adultery, the woman at Jacob's Well—he saw the gift of God in their eyes and said, "There's a prime candidate for forgiveness."

Don't tarry in guilt. Turn to God. He isn't distant like some foreign deity. He comes near as a father saying, "I knew you'd come to me. Now, let me fight that battle with you." We can come back. God is always there.

Thought Questions for Chapter 4

1. Purity is a battleground for Christians in our "glandular society." From 1 Thessalonians 4:1-8, discover at least three reasons we ought to be pure.
2. Read Genesis 2:18-25; 1 Corinthians 7:1-5; Hebrews 13:4; and the Song of Solomon. How would you describe God's view of sex in its proper context?
3. Suppose a Christian teenager came to you asking why he should be sexually chaste. How would you answer?
4. Why is sexual immorality a particularly devastating sin? (Read 1 Corinthians 6:12-20.)

Chapter 5

The Gospel According to the Wall Street Journal

Fyodor Dostoevsky in his novel *The Idiot* dealt with society's craving for wealth and power. The idiot in the novel is a Christ-type character named Prince Myshkin. In a culture much like our own, where nearly everyone hungers and thirsts for wealth, he was a man of integrity. There was no category to describe him, so because he was so unlike everyone else, they thought of him as an idiot.

The people in the days of Jesus must have felt uncomfortable with his lifestyle—a wandering preacher with nothing he could claim as his own. We would probably react the same way. If we didn't know any better, we might call him an idiot.

Rudyard Kipling, speaking to a group of graduates from McGill University, told them not to spend their lives seeking wealth and fortune. If you do, he said, "Someday you will meet a man who cares for none of these things, and then you will know how poor you are."

Materialism is the spirit of our age—both in and out of God's church. You see it in descriptions of people. When someone asks "How much is he worth?" usually the answer is not "More than the whole world because he's made in the image of God," but rather "around 2.5 million dollars." You see it in career decisions made on the basis of financial figures rather than where God wants us to be. You see it in patterns of voting. There's a movement toward conservatism in the United States, not because people are more conservative on specific issues, but because they have more possessions to conserve.

Jay Kesler's insights are right on target:

> I'm amazed how many young people will not look at a car that is not at least BMW quality. They want quality food, quality watches, quality homes, quality enjoyment, quality everything—the best that materialism can buy. . . . If anyone should be able to see through and reject the materialistic philosophy, it should be the Christian church. But I fear we've so adapted ourselves to the cultural norm that we're not in a strong position to lead our youth to a more biblical standard. The church is far quicker to applaud and embrace the "conservative" self-centered values prevalent among youth today than it was to accept the justice-seeking, other-centered idealism of young people in the sixties.

Consider the contrast between Christ and culture when it comes to money. From an advertisement in a national magazine: *"Money!* The gift for people who want everything. How to make money. Invest it more profitably. Spend it more sensibly and pleasurably. Save it prudently and reach financial independence."

What did Jesus say?

> I tell you the truth, it is hard for a rich man to enter the kingdom of heaven. Again I tell you, it is easier for a camel to go through the eye of a needle than for a rich man to enter the kingdom of God (Matthew 19:23).

47

Reverend Ike speaks from a cultural viewpoint. He proclaimed his cultural message wrapped in the aura of the gospel by saying:

> God doesn't want anyone to be poor. If you believe in him, you will believe in yourself. And, if you believe in yourself, you will get rich. I'm rich and that's because I believe in God and I believe in Reverend Ike.

But Jesus said, "Blessed are you who are poor, for yours is the kingdom of God" (Luke 6:20).

From another national news magazine:

> Here's to the dreamers. There are certain people in American business whose motives for working are a bit out of the ordinary. They don't work just to pass the time or to keep food on the table or to pay the mortgage. They're motivated by something more powerful—the American Dream. The dream of turning their brains, their sweat and their talent into a very personal kind of success.

One of Jesus' apostles, however, said,

> But godliness with contentment is great gain. For we brought nothing into the world, and we can take nothing out of it. But, if we have food and clothing, we will be content with that .. . . For the love of money is a root of all kinds of evil (1 Timothy 6:6-8,10).

When we think about culture and its approach to money, two words come to mind: greed and extravagance. Greed is a six-year-old with a sucker looking at a Baskin-Robbins triple scooper. It is a twenty-six-year-old sitting in a Plymouth looking at a Mercedes. It is the middle class family drooling to live in Yuppieville.

On every marquee, through every television screen, inside every popular magazine, greed whines: "You need something else to be full. You lack abundant life until you have this car that talks to you, this watch worth megabucks, this bigger house, this stereo unit." The rhythm beats steadily and stealthily into your skull: "You can— you can have it all." The condo. The trip. The investment.

Greed always cries, "More! More! Give me more!" Paul says that's idolatry (Colossians 3:5). It's like a god. You set money up like a god and it always wants more! It wants extravagance.

There's an ancient Roman proverb that says, "Money is like seawater. The more you drink, the more you want."

J. D. Rockefeller, the richest man of his time, was once asked, "How much money is enough?"

His answer? "Just a little bit more."

You see it everywhere. People want to touch the hem of the garments of Blake Carrington and J. R. Ewing. The person with the $100,000 income may try to touch them by buying a monstrous house that makes him live from check to check. Or the young person who works at Wal-Mart may spend a whole week's salary for a leather jacket that says "Members Only." It's the same principle—they're just coming from different places.

Consider the family where Mom and Dad take more and more jobs. They work weekends and later into the night because they want a bigger house and newer cars. They want their kids to have all the things they couldn't have, though it often makes their kids spoiled and unsatisfied. They work and work while the kids miss the one thing they need—their parents.

Greed and extravagance—those are two words that characterize much of our culture. What two words could we apply to Christ? Obviously, the opposites. One would be contentment, and the other simplicity. The Gospel of Christ is not the "Gospel of Reverend Ike" or the "Gospel of Health and Wealth."

An article in a religious magazine listed twenty-five reasons you might offer someone who's on the verge of becoming a Christian. They included: the most practical way to live, the way to realize success, the best investment of time and money, the way to help your country continue to be Christian, the way to preserve freedom in the USA, a cure for worry, the way to obtain better health and longer life, the way to enjoy financial advantages.

I'd hate to tell somebody to become a Christian for those reasons. What if he knew something about the life of Jesus? He might say, "Well, maybe Jesus wasn't a follower of God, because he wasn't wealthy." What if he knew about Paul? He could turn nearly any place in Second Corinthians and read, "I know what it's like to be without." And what if he knew about the people to whom Hebrews was written? Their property had been plundered.

What about our brothers and sisters in Christ in Western Kenya today? Many of them scrape to get by. They feel starvation from the famine just like everyone else over there. Being disciples of Christ has brought them peace, but not huge homes. What about our brothers and sisters behind the Iron Curtain whose financial position often goes down as their faithfulness to Christ goes up?

Jesus is still the one who said, "You can gain the whole world and lose your soul."

As Carl Henry has said, "The current philosophy 'Be

50

born again and God will put you in clover,' needs divine editing to read, 'Get right with God and he will show you how many excesses you can do without.'"

I described a stereotypical family from culture's perspective. Let me give you one from Christ's perspective. This family is satisfied to live on a modest income in a modest house. The husband passes up several opportunities for job advancement with pay increases because he's happy where he is. They don't have the nicest cars in town. They don't take extravagant vacations. Their kids don't have new stereo equipment, but they all seem happy.

They live a relatively simple life, and they're not judgmental of those who live better. They're content to be where they are. People who know them feel sorry for them. They think, *Old Bob could have done better for himself.* The in-laws think, *If he'd take some of those jobs, they could live in the best part of town. He could be moving up. No telling where he might be in five years.* People think he's ridiculous for the decisions he's made, but he and his family are happy.

Isn't there a limit to the luxuries we can justify? Can people around us see a difference between us and the world at large? Do they notice that we're more modest and live simpler lives, that we don't run out and buy something just because we want it? Is it more important to you to be where you can make a lot of money or where you think God wants you to be? Do you spend more time thinking about God or about a piece of real estate, a house, or a vacation?

Jackson Browne has a song called "The Pretender." It's about a man who began life with great aspirations. He wanted to change things, to do things for people. But his dreams were crushed. All his high ideals plummeted, and he started pursuing material possessions. Listen to what he sings:

I'm going to be a happy idiot
And struggle for the legal tender
Where the ads take aim and lay their claim
To the heart and soul of the spender,
And believe in whatever may lie
In those things that money can buy.
Thought true love could have been a contender
Are you there?
Say a prayer for the pretender
Who started out so young and strong,
Only to surrender.

Dostoevsky's idiot had a simple, satisfying life. Jackson Browne's idiot gave up his ideals to pursue things that will not last. Which one is the true idiot?

Paul gives four insights about money:

1. Contentment and simplicity are essential (1 Timothy 6:6-10). When you start pursuing money outside of godliness, your life will be in trouble. It's godliness with contentment that is great gain. Remember the words of Thoreau: "Simplify, simplify." Or think of Byrd when he was traveling in the Arctic: "I'm learning that a man can live profoundly without masses of things."

Sometimes young couples have marital problems because they can't handle financial matters. They've bought into the world's values, and they've believed they can have everything they want for just so much a month. They've lost track of their responsibility, and it's harming their marriage.

In his book *Celebration of Discipline*, Richard Foster listed ten practical principles for simplifying. These include:

Buy things for their usefulness rather than their status. Apply a bit of healthy skepticism to all "buy now, pay later" schemes. Develop a habit of giving things away. Learn to enjoy things without owning them. Develop a deeper appreciation for things money cannot buy. And shun whatever would distract you from your main goal.

2. Money cannot provide true riches (1 Timothy 6:17-18). The rich man thought possessions could provide happiness, so he built larger and larger barns (Luke 12). Jesus said he was a fool, not because he was rich, but because of his view of possessions. They can never make you contented.

Philip Yancey described his struggle with money. He said, "I finally got to the point through my writing that I had more money than I really needed." That was one of the worst parts of his life, because money started to occupy him and pull him away from the things he really loved.

> Books on investment strategy and tax avoidance tips had supplanted my reading interests in wildlife and classical music. I felt a ceaseless tug to acquire: newer clothes and a bigger house, when those I owned were perfectly adequate; a new car, even though my old one ran fine; a string of investments to accumulate a good nest egg—but for what? Money had become a black hole. The more I had, the more I wanted.

We suffer from the King Midas phenomenon: if we could just turn things into gold, we think, we would be happier. But when we do acquire gold, we often lose the best things in life, which the songs say are free. The modern paradigm was Howard Hughes. The classic example from old was Solomon.

3. Those with money should use it wisely (1 Timothy 6:17-18). Sometimes we go to the opposite extreme and think it's good to be poor and wrong to be rich. That's not what the text says, however. It doesn't say, "Those of you who are rich, deplete all your resources." It says, "Those of you who are rich, use your money wisely."

Society says the richer you are, the more luxuriously you ought to live. The Bible says the richer you are, the more people you can help. If your gift is contributing to the needs of others, give generously (Romans 12:8).

God blesses some people in his church with the spiritual gift of making money so they can bless the world with generosity. Stewardship is the word we usually use. If you have more, you have more to give.

4. The kingdom of God, not things, should be central to our lives (1 Timothy 6:11-16). At the core of our lives should be found, not cars or homes or IRAs, but the kingdom of God. Jesus put it this way: "Seek first the kingdom of God and his righteousness and then all the things you really need will be added to your lives."

Tony Campolo tells of a Mennonite conference debating their historic position that a Christian shouldn't fight in a war. A wealthy old Mennonite gentleman who wanted to be able to protect what he had if anyone invaded his property attacked the position. He was answered by a younger Mennonite. "It's all right for you to talk in this lofty manner," the old gentleman said, "but one of these days they'll come and take everything you have."

The young man responded, "This poses no problem for me. You see, Sir, when I became a Christian, I gave everything I had to Jesus. If they come, they can take from me what belongs to him, and that's his problem."

"All right," the old man responded, "They can't take

what you have because you don't have anything, but they can kill you."

The young man answered, "No, they can't. You see, Sir, I'm already dead. When I became a Christian, the life that belongs to this world came to an end, and the new life that I received in Christ can never be snuffed out."

In frustration, the older man said, "They may not be able to take what you have and they may not be able to kill you, but they can make you suffer."

Once again the young man answered, "When that day comes, I hope I will remember the words of Jesus, who said, 'Blessed are those who are persecuted for righteousness' sake, for theirs is the kingdom of heaven.' You see, Sir, there is not much you can do to somebody who doesn't have anything, who's already dead, and who rejoices in persecution."

If the kingdom of God is at the heart of our lives, we can use the things we have to his glory. It's not right or wrong to be rich or poor. But wherever God has placed you in this life, be sure that you possess your things as a steward of God and that they don't possess you.

Thought Questions for Chapter 5

1. The writer of Hebrews warned us to remain free from the love of money (Hebrews 13:5-6). What does the passage teach us about God that helps produce contentment?
2. Give some examples of how advertisements often seek to instill discontent.
3. Is there a noticeable difference between the lifestyle of Christians and that of non-Christians? Do Chris-

tians typically live with simplicity and contentment?
4. It has been said that America has moved from wanting to be good to wanting to *feel* good. This shifts attention from justice to affluence. Is there evidence that Christians have rejected this shift?

Chapter 6

Sodom Revisited

Forty years ago in polite circles, you did not talk about homosexuality. Forty years ago the churches did not do much more than consider homosexuals to be sick, perverted criminals. Psychiatrists treated them as any other mental patient, while probably millions of people quietly held questions about their sexual preference.

That started to change in 1948. The Kinsey Report issued that year estimated that 37 per cent of the American males had had at least one homosexual experience. That was probably an inflated figure, but homosexuality was and is a large problem in our country.

In 1955 Sherwin Bailey published a book called *Homosexuality in the Western Tradition* in which he reinterpreted biblical passages to say it's against Western tradition and mores, but not against God's will, to be a homosexual. Bailey's book has become the foundation for homosexual theologians.

In the 1960s the Gay Liberation Movement worked to change attitudes.

In 1968, Troy Perry became the pastor of the first openly homosexual church, the Metropolitan Community Church. In 1972, he wrote the book *The Lord Is My Shepherd and He Knows I'm Gay*. Three years later, the

Episcopal Church ordained an avowed lesbian to the ministry.

In April 1985, a homosexual high school opened in New York City, paid for largely by local and state dollars.

The thing that's in most of our minds related to homosexuality is AIDS, the mysterious virus that will claim the lives of thousands more victims because we're incapable of dealing with it at this point.

Homosexuality is a part of our culture. It is something about which we need sound biblical advice. Let's consider it from the standpoint of four questions.

Question number 1: What causes someone to be homosexual? Gary Collins is a psychologist who writes from a Christian perspective. He said,

An increasing body of research would seem to support the idea that homosexuality is not inherited or the result of physiological and biological abnormality. Studies of physical build, chromosomes, neurological or biochemical makeup and even hormones have failed to show differences between homosexuals and heterosexuals. It has been found that while some homosexuals have harmone imbalances, many do not, and a similar hormone imbalance is found in heterosexuals. This has led most researchers to conclude that there is no present evidence to support the idea that homosexuality has a physical or biological cause.

According to Collins, you will usually find certain family settings in the background of homosexuals. The typical homosexual, he says, might be someone raised in a family with a weak, passive, ineffective father and a domineering mother. In such situations, a son often loses confidence in his masculinity. Or the setting might be one in which mothers distrust or fear other women and teach that to their sons. Another typical background consists of mothers who distrust or fear men and teach their daughters to do the same, or of a son who is surrounded only by females and who consequently learns to think and act like a girl. Still another common setting is one in which parents wanted a daughter but got a son and subtly raised him to think like a girl (or vice versa).

Sometimes a son is rejected by his father and feels inadequate as a male, or a daughter is rejected by her mother and feels inadequate as a female. Often both parents are afraid of sex—silent about it in the home except for strong condemnation of sexual feelings. Children get an imbalanced view of sex in that situation.

A person who has learned that behavior from his earliest days is not responsible for his orientation any more than a child who is becoming a heterosexual at age ten can be congratulated for those feelings.

Let's say a child is raised in a family in which stealing is a common event. Both parents steal. His siblings steal. He thinks stealing is a way of life. You cannot say his orientation toward stealing is unusual for that setting. What we can say is that he is still responsible for his behavior.

If homosexuality is a learned thing, we cannot blame the twelve-year-old who has grown up in that setting for his orientation, his predisposition. But we can say biblically that he is responsible for his behavior.

That's where we part company with some behavioral scientists who say you can't go against what you've been taught. Christians believe you *can* control your behavior. There is a distinction between one who has homosexual feelings and temptations and one who is practicing homosexuality. There is no sin involved in homosexual temptation any more than there's sin involve in hetero-sexual temptation. The difference comes when you start giving in to those temptations.

Question number 2: What does scripture say about homosexuality? Genesis 1 says nothing about homosex-uality, and that's significant. "God created man in his own image. In the image of God he created him. Male and female, he created them" (Genesis 1:27). This is God's intent. He made male and female. He did not mean for us to be androgynous.

In Genesis 2, God gave man a woman. He gave man Eve. It was Adam and Eve, not Adam and Steve. God's plan for sexual fulfillment was a marriage between a husband and wife that was to last forever.

Genesis 19 tells of the sin of Sodom. We are told earlier that it is serious. "Now the men of Sodom were wicked and were sinning greatly against the Lord" (Genesis 13:13). "Then the Lord said, 'The outcry against Sodom and Gomorrah is so great and their sins so grievous that I will go down and see if what they've done is as bad as the outcry that has reached me. If not, I will know.'" (Genesis 18:20-21).

He sent his messengers to the city, and when they had eaten and were about to retire, all the men of the city gathered around Lot's house and started screaming, "Bring out the men that we may know them."

Bailey claimed this means only that the men of the city wanted to become acquainted with the messengers. They were a sort of local Welcome Wagon. His evidence for that interpretation was that of the 943 occurrences of *yadhah* ("know") in the Old Testament, only fourteen are clearly sexual.

The determination of a word's meaning, however, comes from its context and not from stacking up numbers of occurrences. "Know" in verse 8 clearly is sexual. It is in verse 5 as well: "We want to have sexual intercourse with the men in your house." The passage stands as a clear condemnation of homosexual activity (cf. Jude 7).

In the New Testament, Paul wrote:

> Don't you know that the wicked will not inherit the kingdom of God? Do not be deceived: Neither the sexually immoral nor idolaters nor adulterers nor male prostitutes nor homosexual offenders nor thieves nor the greedy nor drunkards nor slanderers nor swindlers will inherit the kingdom of God (1 Corinthians 6:9-10).

Those who are practicing acts of homosexuality are condemned by God. It is a sin that can cause you to lose your soul if you do not correct it.

Finally, the book of Romans tells us that the wrath of God was poured out on mankind because of its wickedness.

> Because of this, God gave them over to shameful lusts. Even their women exchanged natural relations for unnatural ones. In the same way the men also abandoned natural relations with women and were inflamed with lust for one another. Men committed indecent acts with other men, and received in themselves the due penalty for their perversion (Romans 1:26).

Question number 3: What should the church's response be to homosexuality? Two words come to mind, confrontation and compassion. The spirit of the age today says I don't have any right to be involved in your life whether you're a Christian or not. You have the right to choose your lifestyle. As one woman's lawyer said in

Oklahoma, "I don't care if she fornicates up one side of the street and down the other, it's none of the church's business."

That's the spirit of the age and of the "Phil Donahue Show," but it is not the spirit of New Testament Christianity. Loving is vital to the New Testament, but not a weak, slimy love. It's a tough love that at times must confront. If I love you and believe what Paul said about homosexuality costing your soul, love will lead me to confrontation.

One way to confront homosexuality is to model good family living. Even single parents can talk positively about people of the opposite sex and present God's plan of sexuality in a positive way.

The second word is compassion. Some Christians need to repent because they have stereotyped people. They have felt that anyone with an effeminate voice is homosexual or that all homosexuals walk the streets looking for little boys to seduce.

Homosexuals need compassion, understanding, and help rather than condemnation and rejection. The church is to love people, not treat them like lepers. We need to repent of our attitudes toward those who honestly struggle with homosexuality.

When Jesus met a sinful woman, he didn't condone her actions, but he was understanding. He tried to minister to her (Luke 7). Some saw her as a leper. They pulled up their pharisaic skirts and tried to walk around her, but Jesus confronted her with compassion.

God calls the church to the same ministry. You can't minister to people you stereotype and write off. Homosexuals need love. The old saying is still valid: "Hate the sin, but love the sinner." Loving confrontation mingled with compassion should characterize the church.

Question number 4: How can the homosexual bring his life under control?

If you're struggling with homosexuality, you *can* control your behavior. It's hard, but it can be done. It's hard for alcoholics to quit drinking—painfully hard. Sometimes they want to be tied down on a bed to keep them from getting another drink. It's hard for someone who's been promiscuous heterosexually for years to stop. What about people who've been stealing all their lives? Do you know how hard it is for them to quit?

It's difficult, but I refuse to buy into the teaching of those who say you can't change. The Bible tells us that God has all power; he can help us develop self-control.

Let me suggest five steps toward recovery. They are painful, difficult, long-term steps, but people have given testimony that with God's help they have become nonpracticing homosexuals.

First, admit that it's a sin. As long as you keep fooling yourself, you have no way to overcome it. People who struggle with homosexuality know the guilt involved with it. Where there is guilt, there is sin, and where there is sin, there is hope. As Paul said, "No temptation has seized you except what is common to man. And God is faithful; he will not let you be tempted beyond what you can bear" (1 Corinthians 10:13).

It isn't that there's no temptation. If you've grown up with that learned behavior, you'll probably be tempted to the day you die, but there will never come a temptation that you cannot choose to combat and overcome by the power of God.

Second, trust in the Lord. I'm not talking about singing or proclaiming that we ought to trust him. We all know that. I mean really turning your life over to him in submission.

There's a being more powerful than we are, and we must rely on him. Homosexuality is a spiritual battle, and we fight it with spiritual weapons (Ephesians 6).

God has a great record. He could take a little David and go up against Goliath. He could take Gideon with 300 men and go up against the myriads of Midianite soldiers. He could take a man with demons and send him to a new life. Homosexuality, like demon-possession, is an overwhelming experience calling for outside help. That help is from God Almighty!

Third, substitute new thoughts and activities for old ones. Break all connections with things that encourage a homosexual orientation—pornography, friendships. Every experience reinforces the chain.

If you're young, don't experiment. Don't play with fire. If you've grown up in environments where you have questions about your orientation, be assured that what God said is true. He made us male and female. Don't change his plan. If you have already had homosexual experiences, don't do it again. Just cut it off.

The mind is not a vacuum. You can't remove all those things and leave it empty. You've got to put new things in. If you don't, you'll go back to the old ways of thinking and acting. Read new material. Find new friends. Associate as much as you can with God's church.

Fourth, confess your orientation to a fellow Christian (James 5:16). That doesn't mean you have to walk down the aisle, fill out a card, and tell the whole community, but share it with somebody.

Finally, believe there is hope. If you don't believe there's hope, there won't be for you. If you believe you're trapped and there's no way out, you're fighting a losing battle.

Earlier in this chapter, we noted that practicing

homosexuals will not inherit the kingdom of God (1 Corinthians 6:9-10). The passage continues, "And that is what some of you were. But you were washed, you were sanctified, you were justified in the name of the Lord Jesus Christ and by the Spirit of our God" (v. 11).

Paul said there were Christians in Corinth who had come out of homosexuality. People there had been mixed up in all the sins we have today, but they had been brought out by the power of the Lord Jesus Christ. That is the hope of the homosexual.

Thought Questions for Chapter 6

1. Describe the typical family background of a homosexual (according to Gary Collins).
2. Explain the difference between a homosexual orientation and homosexual practice.
3. What barriers make it difficult for the church to respond with confrontation and compassion to homosexuals?
4. Brainstorm to list several examples (biblical and nonbiblical) of how great odds were overcome by people who had God's help.

Chapter 7

Disposable Marriages

The *Miami Herald* recently carried an interesting article on marriage:

> A young British couple decided to get a divorce while their wedding reception was still in progress. Daniel and Susan Stockwell had barely started the reception before they had a furious argument that was apparently spurred when the bride saw the groom talking to an ex-girlfriend. "I must have been mad to go through with it!" London's *Daily Merit* newspaper quoted the groom as saying. "I'm better off without her."

While you rarely hear of divorce stemming from the wedding reception, it's not unusual to hear about it not long after. Chuck Swindoll mentioned a sign at a Hollywood pawn shop that said, "We rent wedding rings." Why not? If you aren't going to use it more than a year or two, it would be foolish to pay hundreds or thousands of dollars for a wedding ring. Maybe you could rent with an option to buy later!

At some wedding ceremonies, the words "as long as we both shall live" have been replaced with "as long as we both shall love." Many don't want to enter into contracts for life. Maybe for love, but not for life. For all practical purposes, "until death do we part" has been replaced with "for three years, at which time we'll renegotiate." People want to take another look at things. They don't want a life-long commitment.

The devastation of divorce has even infiltrated the ranks of Christians. We used to say that ninety-nine per cent of the marriages contracted at Christian colleges lasted. We can't say that anymore.

Some who are single may think of marriage as a good thing to try. Notice: *something to try*. If it doesn't work out, just discard it and try again. It's like disposable diapers. Use them, dispose of them, and buy more.

There may seem to be so many exceptions or options on the religious market—so many "outs" to marriage and "ins" for remarriage—that people think, *Well, I'll just try it someday, and if it doesn't work out, I'll try it again with someone else.*

Holiness demands that we stand against the cultural tide. We must try to transform culture rather than just ride along with it. Our views of marriage need to be carved out of Scripture and out of Jesus' view of marriage regardless of what they're doing on "Hill Street Blues," what a Gallup Poll says, or what *People* magazine advocates (with articles like "How to Marry and Stay Married" by Elizabeth Taylor).

Of course, you can be divorced and still be a faithful Christian. You don't have to be a second-class citizen in God's kingdom just because you're divorced. God loves all his children, and he heals all wounds.

Some of the most sensitive, compassionate people in the world are people who have been divorced. They would probably be the first to say that divorce isn't God's plan for marriage. The trials and upheavals they experienced cannot be God's plan.

God's Design for Marriage

Out of all the creatures, only one was found fit for Adam—woman, the one God specially made (Genesis 2:21). He brought them together and said to Adam, "Cleave to your wife. Be united with her." There's something permanent about that. God wasn't saying, "Adam, try Eve for a while and then start looking around." For one thing, the pickin's were pretty slim at the time! Rather, God said, "Cleave to her. Stay with her." God wants one man and one woman united for life. This concept of cleaving is important. God's design for marriage is permanent.

The life of Hosea was intertwined with the message of God's love for Israel. The tragedies the Lord was experiencing with his people, Israel, were the same tragedies Hosea was experiencing with his wife.

Hosea had what we call a scriptural reason for divorce. His wife had left him. She was an adulteress. She played the field. But Hosea still wanted her back. Just because adultery is involved doesn't mean you have to divorce. That's how sacred marriage was to God and to Hosea. God said to Hosea, "Go out and find your wife again and bring her back" (Hosea 3:1). That's the way God loved Israel.

God's love for Israel is eternal. It's a love that keeps pursuing. It's a tough kind of love. That's the kind of love he wanted Hosea, and us, to have.

Malachi was God's last call to his people in the Old Testament. He called them to come back to him, to quit abusing the poor and downtrodden. He called for justice.

> Another thing you do: You flood the Lord's altar with tears. You weep and wail because he no longer pays attention to your offerings or accepts them with pleasure from

your hands. You ask, "Why?" It is because the Lord is acting as the witness between you and the wife of your youth,
because you have broken faith with her, though she is your
partner, the wife of your marriage covenant. Has not the
Lord made them one? In flesh and spirit they are his. And
why one? Because he was seeking godly offspring. So
guard yourself in your spirit, and do not break faith with
the wife of your youth. "I hate divorce," says the Lord God
of Israel . . . . (Malachi 2).

That's unequivocal! There aren't a lot of ways to
interpret it. God hates divorce. Despite all the exceptions we might talk about and the special cases we might
come up with, the bottom line is God's design, beginning
in Genesis and continuing through Malachi: God wants
marriage to be permanent.

Jesus reiterated the emphasis on permanence.
Loophole lawyers are always looking for an "out," an
excuse why this doesn't apply. But Jesus didn't negotiate
with loophole lawyers. He said, "Yes, fornication is a way
of breaking the bond." But he returned to the heart of
long-term commitment:

Haven't you read, he replied, that at the beginning the Creator "made them male and female," and said, "For this reason a man will leave his father and mother and be united to
his wife, and the two will become one flesh"? So they are no
longer two, but one. Therefore what God has joined together, let man not separate (Matthew 19:4-6).

Finally, Paul used marriage as an illustration when he
said,

For example, by law a married woman is bound to her
husband as long as he is alive, but if her husband dies, she

is released from the law of marriage. So then, if she marries another man while her husband is still alive, she is called an adulteress. But if her husband dies, she is released from that law and is not an adulteress, even though she marries another man (Romans 7:2-3).

God wants marriage to last for life. There will be ups and downs, but he wants us to stay in there with stubborn love. Don't focus on exceptions. Look at God's design for marriage. God has always said, "I want people to stay married for life."

Preventative Measures

We've got to buck the cultural tide of disposable marriages. Holiness demands it. If we're going to be God's people, we have to find a way for our marriages to last and be a light to the world. The following are seven preventative measures that can help you preserve your marriage.

1. Love even when you don't feel like loving. We're in trouble if we marry with love as a feeling, because feelings are fickle. Most of the time, they're good and warm. But, other times, they aren't. You can't rely on them.

Love is a command. You can't command feelings, but you can command commitment. So when Paul said, "Husbands, love your wives," he wasn't saying have a romantic feeling 365 days a year. He was telling us to make a decision that you're going to love.

Jesus said to love your enemies (Matthew 5). He wasn't saying to have tickly feelings on the inside about them. He was calling for a basic commitment of good will toward them.

We need the kind of committed love expressed in a note

Charlie Shedd's wife left him after an argument: "Dear Charlie, I hate you. Love, Martha." We who are married can identify!

You can't always deal with the emotions, but you can deal with decisions. "I've decided I'm going to love you. Even on days we don't feel particularly close, I'm going to act lovingly toward you." And as you act that way, the feelings will eventually follow. You're not trying to do something against your will. You want to love. You want to make that commitment for life. That's a healthy view of love.

2. *Zero in on positive qualities.* Paul in his epistles always began by talking about things for which he was thankful. He was almost always writing to correct something, but he began with something positive. Even in his first epistle to the Corinthians, when he could hardly think of anything good to say, he thanked God for "the grace that is evident among you." God was working among them whether they knew it or not.

Sandra Milholland penned these insightful words in *Upreach* magazine:

Ladies, beware of those "coffee klatches" with the girls in the neighborhood or on your coffee break at work. I have noticed that husbands often get skewered, cooked and eaten at those gatherings (figuratively speaking, of course), and a ten o'clock gab session in the morning can have a subtle but powerful impact on how a wife will treat her husband in the evening. Sue complains about her husband, Gretchen complains about hers and others join in with similar complaints. Agreeing that "men are all alike," everyone feeds on everyone else's grievances.

I would like to challenge us to break that truly vicious cycle. Begin by spending time thinking warm thoughts about your husband, and the next time your friends want to play

71

"Ain't Hubby Awful," let your responses be only positive ones. Build him up in the eyes of others. As his strengths come to mind, flaunt them! Guys, I'm talking to you too. When other men complain about their "little missus," march to the beat of a different drummer and praise your woman. After all, she did have the good sense to marry you, didn't she?

Focus on the positive qualities. Look for the good things in your mate. What drew you together in the first place? Those may be the things that irritate you now. Before marriage he seemed so decisive, and you liked that. Now he seems pigheaded. It's the same quality from a different perspective!

3. Reserve time for each other. It's so easy to get caught up in all the things we're doing—speaking here, working overtime there, taking on an extra responsibility—and before you know it, you start to get subtle hints that you haven't been home enough. For example, you drive up in your driveway and hear one of your kids yell, "Mommie, some man wants to see you!"

James Dobson wrote about a busy gynecologist whose wife was having abdominal pains. This OB-GYN called another OB-GYN who was a friend of Dobson's. "You know, my wife's got some terrible abdominal pains," the husband said. "I don't know what's wrong, and I hate to see her myself. I'm so busy, and I don't want to see my own wife in that sense anyway. So, would you mind treating her?"

The doctor visit revealed that the lady was five months pregnant! Her own OB-GYN spouse hadn't figured it out. "I must admit wondering how in the world this woman ever got his attention long enough to conceive," Dobson wrote.

A husband and wife can drift apart so easily. You get busy and you don't see as much of each other. Before you know it, your marriage is suffering. Companionship and communication *must* be priorities for us.

4. Avoid situations that hinder the relationship. Careers are great, but if careers draw us away from our marriages, we need to opt for the marriage rather than the career. If my career is demanding more and more time, if I have to move frequently and be away from home a lot, if the kids don't know me and my wife and I never have time to talk, I may need to sacrifice my career. It's better to live in a warm apartment than a cold mansion.

I may have to give up some acquaintances. If I have friends who talk about how great divorce is or how much they enjoy running around on their wives, and if I start feeling that pull, I need to avoid those friends.

A hobby could be the culprit. I may enjoy the hobby, and my wife may want me to have it. But if my participation interferes with our needed time together, I ought to give it up.

You may be in situations at work where you feel sexually enticed. You may see a woman every day who hasn't had to deal with kids the first thing in the morning. She may look nice all the time. If you start feeling burdened with temptation, you may need to sacrifice being around her for the sake of your marriage.

5. Accept part of the blame when things are going wrong. Sometimes in marriage we think it's all the other person's fault. "I haven't done anything wrong. I've tried to patch things up. Everything's your fault."

It's like the "ring around the collar" detergent commercial on TV. She's crying. Her detergent has failed. She's failed. She's worthless. She's no good. But the commercial never asks the most important question, "Why doesn't the pig ever wash his neck?"

So maybe our prayer should not be, "Lord, change my spouse," but "Lord, change me."

6. *Call for help if you need it.* It's very un-American to call for help—and very biblical. We tend to think that we can't let our defenses down and confess that we have problems because other people don't. There may be a stigma attached to admitting we have problems.

The Bible says to call for help, to admonish one another, serve one another, confess to one another. There's something very biblical about saying "I need help."

It's terrible to hear a divorce announced and be taken by surprise. Maybe we were ignorant, but more often the people involved were too proud to admit they were struggling in their marriage. If you're at some kind of crisis point in your marriage and you know you need help, *ask for it.*

Many churches have special programs to help families in trouble. There are many people who've been trained to assist you. Don't be afraid to seek assistance.

7. *Keep your marriage centered on God.* This is of paramount importance. Someone contemplating marriage must determine to find someone whose spiritual pilgrimage is taking him or her closer to God. Paul said there are two kinds of people in the world—Christians and non-Christians (1 Corinthians 2). Even among Christians there are two kinds of people—carnal Christians and spiritual Christians (1 Corinthians 3). Find someone who is spiritually minded, not just an immersed pagan. Find somebody who's committed to God.

Ask these three questions: Do I see in this person a desire to be God's man or woman? Does this person have a deep prayer life? Does being with this person bring me closer or pull me farther from God?

A lot of things won't matter after fifteen years. How well he plays basketball or sings in the choir won't really matter. How beautiful her hair is is not nearly so important. But after a decade and a half, it is important that this person love God with all his heart, soul, and mind.

The last question we need to ask is, Am I the kind of person who's trying to be God's man or woman? If you're married, are you aiding the marriage spiritually? If you're contemplating marriage, will you build it up and bring your spouse closer to God? Is there a richness to your prayer life? Are you feeding (or will you feed) your spouse and children? The ability to say yes to those questions is the greatest gift you could give your family.

Thought Questions for Chapter 7

1. Divorce is a significant problem in God's church today. Too many marriages are unraveling. Try to identify some of the main causes of this problem.
2. Communication has been called "the life blood of marriage." What modern pressures work against the desperate need for communication and time together?
3. Read 1 Corinthians 13. Write out your own definition of love—the kind of love that is not affected by feelings.
4. In "Fiddler on the Roof," Tevye says to his Jewish daughter who is about to marry a Gentile: "A bird and a fish may love one another, but where would they build a nest?" Apply this to the importance of marrying a dedicated Christian.

Chapter 8

Secular Humanism

When an Arabic sheik's four sons returned from studying at a Western university, he took them on a trip through the desert to discover what they had learned. Coming upon a pile of bones, he asked his first son, "Son, what did you learn?"

"Those are the bones of a six-foot, 300-pound lion," the young man said.

The father was impressed. He asked his second son, "Son, what did you learn?" And that son took the bones and assembled them back into the carcass of a lion.

When he asked the third son the same question, he took the hide and put it over the frame of the lion.

When he finally asked the fourth son what he had learned, he touched the lion and gave it life. Then the lion rose up and ate all five of them.

That's a parable of what takes place today in Western society when we delve into ways of thinking that can destroy us.

Secular humanism has been called the intellectual spirit of the age. Its influence is keenly felt in the United States; it comes across subtly through the media, and specifically at many universities in our land. Indeed, many people who don't know what secular humanism is

76

live with some of its presuppositions because they've been fed them without realizing it.

Before we examine secular humanism in detail, we need to do some qualifying:

1. Not all humanism is secular. Humanism strives for the dignity of man—to help man be all he can be. That isn't anti-Christian. In fact, it's very biblical. Humanists who have striven through the centuries to give dignity to man from a Christian perspective include Justin Martyr, Origen, Augustine, Thomas Aquinas, Erasmus, John Calvin, Alexander Campbell, C. S. Lewis, and J. R. R. Tolkien.

2. Not all goals of secular humanism are bad. Some things the secular humanists are trying to do are good. For example, they promote freedom—sounding much like the founding fathers of the United States, who were not exactly evangelical Christians themselves. Many of them were deists, children of Rousseau and Voltaire. They believed in a god, but not a god who was intervening in the world.

Secular humanists oppose racism, hatred, injustice, inhumanity, poverty, and war. In fact, at times they sound more like Amos, Isaiah, and Jeremiah than conservative Christians do. Often we bury our heads in upper middle class values, leaving others to speak out on issues we should be addressing.

3. Secular humanism is not the greatest battle most of us will face. It's more likely that we'll be materialists, with our greatest goal in life being to have a six-figure income and drive a fancy car, than that we'll be secular humanists. Nevertheless, secular humanism is a serious concern. It just needs to be put into perspective.

The Humanist View of Reality

The central presupposition of secular humanism is its view of reality: "the essence of reality is nature; matter is all there is." Frederick Edwards wrote in *Humanist* magazine, "We base our understanding of the world on what we can perceive with our senses and what we can comprehend with our minds." In other words, they use only empirical, or sensory, evidence to ascertain what is true. You only believe what you can see and touch.

Christianity, on the other hand, says that not only is there the natural, but there is also the supernatural.

In 1933, the Humanist Manifesto was written. In 1973, the second Humanist Manifesto said, "We find insufficient evidence for the existence of the supernatural." This presupposition about reality leaves no place for God and says that the universe is eternal. As Carl Sagan said in his public televison series, "The cosmos is all that is or ever was or ever will be."

Astrophysicist Robert Jastrow pointed out that the study of thermodynamics as well as the study of radiation show that there must have been a beginning. There was some kind of big bang, whether it was the creative force of God or something else. He doesn't know what caused it, but he says matter is not eternal. That's a real problem for secular humanists.

Jastrow described it this way: The scientists have been using their empirical tools for years, scaling the mountains of ignorance, and all of a sudden, they get to the last peak, they reach above to find their own personal answers, and there they're greeted by theologians who have been waiting for them for centuries.

Secular humanists say man is matter, nothing but the chemicals that make up his body. Christianity says man is not only flesh, but he's also spirit. There's something

God has breathed into the soul of man that sets him apart from the rest of creation. He shares personality with God.

Some secularists imply that there are no absolute morals, that all is relative. You cannot absolutely say that this is right and that is wrong, they assert, because such judgment implies an intelligent being in the universe. Christianity says there is a God, and since he has spoken, there are some absolute morals.

Christians and secular humanists part company on the question of the afterlife as well. Secular humanism believes there is none. When you die, your existence is over. Christianity says there are both heaven and hell.

The beliefs of the secular humanists are at least consistent. Given their presupposition that all in the universe is matter or nature, their conclusions fall into place. There could not be a God. You'd have to say that the universe was eternal. Man would be nothing but the dust of which he's made. All morals would be relative, and there would not be an afterlife.

On the other hand, beginning with the Christian presupposition that there is not only a natural realm but a supernatural one as well, the conclusions of Christianity are also consistent. There is a God who created the universe. He created man with a soul. There are moral absolutes because God has spoken propositionally, and there is an afterlife where he rewards those who are his disciples and punishes those who are not.

For a while I thought Christians operated by faith while scientists operated by knowledge—wrong knowledge, perhaps, but knowledge nonetheless. But Don England points out in his excellent book **A Scientist Examines Faith and Evidence** that we *all* begin with faith. Secular humanists may deny it, but the presupposition that all that exists is nature is a statement of faith. How could they know that? Not by empirical study, because empirical study isn't adequate to discover the supernatural realm.

Sir Arthur Eddington told of a fisherman who went out with a special net to prove that no fish are less than two inches long. When he published his study, his colleagues were overwhelmed. "How can you say that?" they asked. "Of course there are fish less than two inches. Maybe it's your net. Look at the holes in your net." Sure enough, the holes in his net were two inches wide. All the small fish were slipping through.

That's what the secular humanists do. They declare that nothing exists that they can't find empirically. That's their statement of faith. But their empirical studies aren't going to discover God, because you can't put God into a test tube.

Walter Cronkite was not there to cover creation. You couldn't have read about it in the newspaper. Nobody was there as an eyewitness, and you can't reproduce it in a lab. It's a statement of faith to say that all that exists is physical.

The secular humanists say that time plus chance plus matter came together to form this world. They admit that the odds against that are incredible, but their faith tells them that everything that exists is a part of nature. My faith tells me, however, that there *is* the possibility of a supernatural realm.

Paul treated the problem of division in the church in Corinth by pointing out a faulty view of wisdom. Some people were buying into the Athenian view that wisdom is a matter of rationalizing, of man's knowledge. Paul didn't discount that kind of thinking, but he raised the possibility that that's not all there is to wisdom.

We do, however, speak a message of wisdom among the mature, but not the wisdom of this age or of the rulers of this age, who are coming to nothing. No, we speak of God's secret wisdom, a wisdom that has been hidden and that God destined for our glory before time began (1 Corinthians 2:6-7).

The rulers of the age didn't know about it. They were looking for something physical, not metaphysical. They weren't going to find it, because it's not a part of nature. It's a matter of revelation. It's not subject to empirical study. "The eye has not seen, the ear has not heard, the mind has not conceived what God has prepared for those who love him."

As a believer, I choose to live based on evidence I think is sufficient regarding God's work in this world. Where do I find it? From man? No, if you want to find out about man, ask man. If you want to find out about God, ask God. The spirit of God reveals the things of God. Man can know some things about God innately, but not everything. God reveals himself. Only the man of the spirit who is open to the possibility of revelation can discern God's truths.

"The spiritual man makes judgments about all things," Paul said. Don't throw out the results of man's reasoning. We're not trying to be anti-intellectual. However, we must accept not only the physical but also the metaphysical, not only the natural but also the supernatural.

We can buy into the world view of secular humanism without even knowing it. When we deny that God is working today, when we fail to talk about him or to recognize his fruit in the life of a fellow Christian, we're buying into the presupposition of secular humanism—that all that exists is matter.

Paul told us to open our eyes—there is more to this world than flesh. The proof is the cross of Christ. It's not something you know by empirical research, because empirically, it looks like a failure. It's "foolishness to Gentiles and a stumbling block to Jews." When you look at the cross with natural perception, all you see is a Jew dying senselessly. He had a good following, a good beginning, and he could have done well. But it ended in tragedy.

The cross is not foolishness, however, when you look beyond to the spiritual dimension.

> He chose the lowly things of this world and the despised things—and the things that are not—to nullify the things that are, so that no one may boast before him. It is because of him that you are in Christ Jesus, who has become for us the wisdom from God—that is, our righteousness, holiness and redemption (1 Corinthians 1:28-30).

Christians launch out in faith, claiming that there is more to life than nature. It's not a blind leap, but a reasoned one. It knows by experience that God is working today. It sees evidence that there's more to life than matter. You can't prove it in a science lab, but when you're near death, you probably won't have a lab available.

Walking with God is crucial to the life of a Christian so that he can testify to those around him, "I know God is acting today! I've walked through the valleys with him and lived on the mountains with him, and I know he's working providentially in this world."

Walking with God shows us that our presuppositions are right. It's not just a matter of feeling. I have evidence on which to base my faith. In the dark valleys of life, philosophy doesn't do a lot of good, nor does empirical knowledge. But my faith in a God who is working in this world does.

Consequences of Secular Humanism

Not everyone who claims to be a secular humanist subscribes to its logical consequences, just as not everyone who claims to believe in God lives as if he exists. But there are three consequences of secular humanism that are examples of where it leads:

1. Moral relativism. Moral relativism means that there are not absolute statements. You can't say that adultery is always wrong, sometimes it may be right. You cannot say that murder is always wrong, because while usually it is wrong, it might sometimes be right in certain circumstances.

Christianity says there is a God who has spoken through his word, and we *can* make moral statements. In the Ten Commandments—not, as someone has pointed out, the Ten Suggestions—God says absolutely, "This is to be the way with my people" (Exodus 20:2-17).

They are commandments—things to do and not to do. We don't judge them against the situation, weigh one view against the other, and end up some place in the middle. Some points in life are vague, but others are unequivocal. God has clearly spoken.

Secular humanists promote justice and attack racism. Christianity does, too. Because God made the people around me, I have a basis for loving them. It's rooted in our love for God.

Secular humanism, on the other hand, promotes the same agenda without the basis. Elton Trueblood called ours a "cut flower" civilization—where you try to hold to the agenda of Christianity (loving your fellow man) without the roots of Christianity. A society that promotes loving man without starting out by loving God is like a cut flower. Over a period of time it fades and dies, because loving man must be rooted in loving God.

Secular humanists say there are no moral absolutes until you impinge on their territory. In July of 1984, Bryant Gumble interviewed Hugh Hefner on the "Today" show. It was right after *Penthouse* magazine published nude photos of Vanessa Williams, who was Miss America at the time. *Penthouse* was selling well, and *Playboy* was suffering. Hefner said *Penthouse* was morally wrong because Miss Williams had not posed for the purpose of having the photos published! Hefner has implied for years that there are no moral absolutes, but when it impinged on his business, he changed his mind.

Some people have championed sexual choice and sexual freedom. They say you need to throw off your old sexual mores, the limitations of religion. You should not be held back. That's a moral statement. They're saying it's morally wrong to tell someone it's morally wrong to be sexually free. What a contradiction!

The same thing occurs when secular humanists feel they're being lied to. They condemn it. Upon what basis? They might say, "Well, it's against society's values." What about Hitler? What he did was not against his society's values. Given the teachings of *Mein Kampf,* Hitler was consistent. Pogroms are consistent with racial bigotry. The Allies at the Nuremberg Trials didn't appeal to the laws of Germany or Great Britain or the United States. They appealed to a higher law.

Everyone has moral absolutes, but Christians know where they come from. They're rooted in the first and greatest commandment—to love God.

2. A lack of regard for life. Humanists seek the dignity of man, but secular humanists don't know how. Man is created in the image of God (Genesis 1:27). But B. F. Skinner, a secular humanist, said, "Not like God. More like a dog!" Man, for Skinner, is just like Pavlov's dog. He responds to the right stimuli. If you feed him the right things, he'll respond the right way.

In his book *The Great Evangelical Disaster,* Francis Schaeffer discussed this low view of man:

> When one accepts the secular world view that the final reality is only material or energy shaped by chance, then human life is lowered to the level of animal existence. There are only two classifications—nonlife and life. And if one thinks of human life as basically no different from animal life, why not treat people the same way? It would only be religious nostalgia to do otherwise. And so it first becomes easy to kill children in the womb, and then if one does not like the way they turn out, to kill children after they're born. . . . After all, according to the secular world view, human life is not intrinsically different from animal life—so why should it be treated differently?

Abortion is a good example of the logical consequences of secular humanism. It's promoted in the second Humanist Manifesto. If you discount passages like Genesis 1 and Psalm 139, then abortion is judged only on expediency. Since Rowe vs. Wade in 1973, it's been expedient over 13,000,000 times in our country. Two years ago Peter Singer wrote in favor of abortion in the *Journal of Pediatrics:* "Only the fact that the defective infant is a member of this species, **homo sapiens,** leads it to be treated differently from the dog or pig. Species membership alone, however, is not morally relevant."

3. A naive view of man. Some secular humanists—

particularly those in America—are optimistic about man. If we can just train men better, they will be better. If we treat them better, we can wipe out poverty, war, and racial injustice. Man is limited, not because of anything moral, but because he just hasn't evolved far enough yet.

Man's real problem, however, is moral (Genesis 3). Man and woman rebelled against God. "The heart is deceitful above all things and beyond cure. Who can understand it?" (Jeremiah 17:9). *The problem of man, his central limitation, is not that he doesn't know what to do but that he knows and chooses to do evil anyway.*

Dostoevsky lived in nineteenth-century Russia among idealists who had a romantic view that men were changing for the better. Dostoevsky wrote time and again to emphasize the place of sin. He wrote in *Notes from the Underground* that everyone says that the fact that man is getting better is as plain as 2 plus 2 equals 4. But Dostoevsky said that when you're dealing with man, it's more accurate to say 2 plus 2 is sometimes 5, because man doesn't always act logically. "Man everywhere and always, whoever he may be, has preferred to act as he wished and not in the least as his reason and advantage dictated," Dostoevsky said.

Christians go back to the early chapters of Genesis and read about the Fall and to the New Testament to see the redeeming work of Christ. He came, not to educate us, not to polish the rough edges, but to deal with moral problems. He died for our sins. We struggle with that. We know what to do, and we don't do it (Romans 7). Paul concluded, "Oh, wretched man that I am! Who can deliver me? Thank God through Jesus Christ our Lord! There's no condemnation for those who are in Jesus Christ."

	SECULAR HUMANISM	CHRISTIANITY
*Reality	Nature	Nature + Supernatural
God	Doesn't exist	Exists
Universe	Eternal	Created
Man	Matter	Matter + Soul
Morals	Relative	Absolute
Afterlife	Doesn't exist	Heaven & Hell

Thought Questions for Chapter 8

1. Explain what Elton Trueblood meant by "a cut flower civilization." In what way can Christians provide roots?
2. What does it mean for Christians to "walk by faith"? Does the lack of absolute, scientific evidence keep us from holding our beliefs with certainty?
3. In 1 Corinthians 1-4, Paul addressed the problem of division by investigating a faulty view of wisdom. What limitations did he place on worldly wisdom?
4. How can we prepare our children for a world that often operates by secularist presuppositions?

Chapter 9

"Chumming the Waters"

My first experience trolling for king mackerel off the East Coast was like a chapter out of some exotic fairytale. My wife, Diane, and I were with our good friends Joe and Kathy Mattox in their comfortable boat. The weather was gorgeous: bright sun, soft breeze, minuscule waves. It was the kind of day where you almost hope the fish will leave you alone (almost!).

When Joe invited me to go tournament fishing with him, I thought that since it was so much fun on just a regular day, there was no telling how much fun a tournament would be. But an amazing transformation can come over a man when you pass from a regular, mess-around day to a bona fide tournament day. Laid Back, Who-Cares-If-You-Missed-One Joe turns into Joe the Zealot. (Maybe that is part of why he is well-known for his tournament fishing on the East Coast!)

We began (in biblical terminology) during the second watch of the night. We got up before intelligent people normally do and went up and down the Intracoastal Waterway looking for baitfish. On a nontournament day any baitfish will do, but on a tournament day it has to be menhaden, about six inches long—just what a mackerel is looking for when its tummy is empty. When we found them flipping in the water, Joe threw the net and hauled in three or four hundred fish, enough for the day.

On the previous day, we'd gotten about the same number of menhaden and had fed them into a meat grinder. You can imagine how much fun that was—for me and the menhaden! You also can imagine the smell the next morning after it sat out half-frozen the previous night. This menhaden mush was put in a sack and became our chum bag. Now with the chum bag plus the live menhaden, out we went to the ocean. This time there was no sun shining and the waves were nasty as we headed seaward forty or fifty miles.

When we finally reached *the* spot, we tossed the chum bag out. Then we began trolling around it in circles. But to make the area even more enticing to a king mackerel, we (actually—*I*) continued dicing the live menhaden into thirds and tossing the pieces behind the boat as fresh chum. That ranks on the excitement scale right up there with changing a baby's diapers, gargling warm salt water, and having a cavity filled.

With the chum bag out and fresh chunks of menhaden in the water, there is often a feeding frenzy. Word gets out that there are freebies floating on the water surface, and every mackerel and shark within a wide radius shows up for a meal. (The similarities to a college student taking a pizza into his dormitory room are striking.) Up come the mackerel, and if you're lucky, they start hitting the bait on your line.

This method of fishing is analogous to a style of evangelism Paul described.

But thanks be to God, who always leads us in triumphal procession in Christ and through us spreads everywhere the fragrance of the knowledge of him. For we are to God the aroma of Christ among those who are being saved and those who are perishing. To the one we are the smell of death; to the other, the fragrance of life. And who is equal to such a task? Unlike so many, we don't peddle the word of God for profit. On the contrary, in Christ we speak before God with sincerity, like men sent from God (2 Corinthians 2:14-17).

The two concepts we're considering in this study of Christ and culture are holiness and ministry. The first eight chapters centered on holiness—how we can be distinct in our values from the world. The remaining chapters concern our ministry—how we infiltrate a world in darkness with the light of the Gospel, how we identify without becoming identical, how we function as fishers of men.

A Chum Bag for the World

We serve as chum—a chum bag that's set out for the world. Not a very glamorous position, is it? Thomas a Kempis said, "God has lots of people who are yearning for the kingdom, but not nearly so many who are willing to bear the cross."

One of my favorite religious novels was written by Sheldon VanAuken. He and his wife, Davie, considered themselves "high pagans." They were not believers, but they lived fairly moral lives. After they moved to England and began rubbing elbows with C. S. Lewis, they came to believe that Jesus was who He claimed to be. In his book *A Severe Mercy*, VanAuken reflected on the conversion process:

The best argument for Christianity is Christians: their joy, their certainty, their completeness. But the strongest argument against Christianity is also Christians—when they are somber and joyless, when they are self-righteous and smug in complacent consecration, when they are narrow and repressive, then Christianity dies a thousand deaths.

It's inescapable. If you've claimed Christ, you're part of the chum—either the best argument Christianity could have or the worst. Either you're the smell of life or the smell of death. There's no in-between. That's God's strategy for reaching people—to throw the chum bag out and keep cutting up people and pouring them out so others will smell and come to the ultimate bait.

That's what Jesus did: "The Word became flesh and lived for a while among us. We have seen his glory, the glory of the one and only son, who came from the Father, full of grace and truth" (John 1:14). Jesus didn't just bring grace and truth, he embodied it in his life. When you touched him, you were touching mercy. You were touching love like you'd never fathomed before, so you caught a glimpse of grace.

Jesus brought grace and truth. He was ground up in the meat grinder, because God was drawing people. He wanted them to smell the fragrance of the love he had from eternity, so he set apart Christ before the worlds were made so he might be the sacrificial lamb. Jesus knew how to identify without becoming identical, and we are called to the same today.

Paul discussed how to minister to a culture that is different from you in his first letter to the church at Thessalonica:

Make it your ambition to lead a quiet life, to mind your own business and to work with your hands, just as we told you, so that your daily life may win the respect of outsiders and so that you will not be dependent on anybody (1 Thessalonians 4:11-12).

How do you win this respect? By marching up and down the streets of Thessalonica? Paul said, "Just live good, Christlike lives, and before they're aware of it, those around you will let down some of their defenses."

But how do you react when people persecute you? Do you retaliate? Give up on your faith? Peter wrote to encourage Christians who are being slandered:

Dear friends, I urge you, as foreigners and strangers in this world, to abstain from sinful desires, which war against your soul. Live such good lives among the pagans that, though they accuse you of doing wrong, they may see your good deeds and glorify God on the day he visits us (1 Peter 2:11-12).

Peter continued by encouraging Christians to obey the law, to put in a good day's work, to accept any persecution that comes. He told wives of non-Christians to demonstrate the beauty of knowing Christ, to be submissive, to keep serving and loving. He told husbands not to treat their wives as second-class citizens but to be considerate of them and fill them with self-esteem. And he told everyone not to bicker but to live in harmony and repay evil with good.

When you live good, integrated lives like that, someone will ask you about the hope you have. At that point, very gently, you tell him the story of Jesus.

What would you need to see in a church? Love. "This is the way all people will know you are my disciples, if you love one another" (John 13:35).

If people out there see a diverse people who are still

united in love, they stop and take notice. This is the badge of discipleship. Francis Schaeffer called it "the final apologetic."

Chum and Churches

Consider two hypothetical churches. Church number 1 is heavy on doctrine. The people there want to be right, and they want others to know they're right. Attendance is about 200 on Sunday morning, which is where it's been for more than twenty years. On Sunday night it drops to about 110, and on Wednesday night it goes down to about 95. Those who don't make it to every service are regularly scolded in the bulletin and from the pulpit.

Decisions are made with very little communication other than to tell the members what's been decided. The leaders know they are to edify, so they have three regular assemblies each week plus a potluck once a month. They know they should be involved in benevolence, so they keep a clothes room stocked with worn out, old-fashioned clothes no one wanted anyway.

For evangelism, they make plain to others in the community how distinctive they are in using the Bible. Their advertising tells others why they're wrong, as do most of the sermons in the assembly. Two gospel meetings are held faithfully every year.

Bickering is common, often over minor issues. The members are well-known in the community for their inability to get along.

Now, church number 2 also emphasizes doctrine, but it is doctrine that grows out of an intimate relationship with God. Attendance on Sunday morning is also about 200, but it's up forty from two years ago. Nearly 175 come back on Sunday evenings, and almost that many on

Wednesday night. No one harangues them about going; they just want to.

Nearly 90 per cent of the members can identify how they fit into the work of the church. They feel a part of it, and decision-making involves communication and input. Edifying is done in the assembly with a sense of excitement, and lessons are geared toward nourishment and growth. Smaller groups meet through the month to discuss problems and triumphs more personally.

The congregation actively seeks to minister to the community. They buy a pair of jeans for any school child needing them. They assist in job training and placement for the unemployed. They regularly sit down with people going through emotional and physical pain. Evangelism for them is a natural part of that kind of serving. Just as they are concerned about the bodies and minds of others, so they care about their souls. They go to people seeking truth together as friends should.

Sometimes they disagree in the church, but overall people can't help but notice "how they love one another."

Two churches—both are chum. One is the chum of death in a community. It's the worst argument you could have for Christianity. The other is the chum of life, and you'll never find a more powerful apologetic.

Chum and the Individual Christian

What does the world need to see in the life of an individual Christian? First, people need to see that we're convicted of God's grace, that we realize we can never be good enough on our own. I go out with hope knowing that the grace of God empowers me, saves me, and motivates me to share with other people.

Second, people need to see sincerity. Have you seen a Christian who is found to have lied to public officials or been involved in an affair or is known around town as a gossip or as a person who cuts sharp corners on business deals? Integrity is the operative word. Sincerity. Being true chum.

Finally, people should see us emphasizing what's really important—exalting family life and simple spirituality—not believing what television tells us we have to have to be happy.

Paul told us what kind of individual we need to deploy into the world, what kind of congregation can sit out there as a chum bag and be fragrance to all the people around. "And we, who with unveiled faces all reflect the Lord's glory, are being transformed into his likeness with ever-increasing glory, which comes from the Lord, who is the Spirit" (2 Corinthians 3:18).

Through the intimate growth that comes by gazing at Jesus Christ, it's as if the Word had become flesh again. We identify with our culture, and they see grace and truth.

God takes us out in the boat. He grinds us up and throws us back into the waters as chum. When people around us take a whiff, is it the aroma of Christ or the stench of death? You're either the best or the worst argument Christianity has.

Thought Questions for Chapter 9

1. What implications does the following statement have for your life?
   "The crucified savior can be communicated best through the life of a crucified servant." (Jim Woodroof)
2. Which of the following best represents your view of the world?

95

    a) "A Philistine camp I should avoid."

    b) "An enemy outpost I should destroy."

    c) "A tunnel of darkness I should enlighten."

3. In what sense is love "the final apologetic"? If it is, how good a case have we made for Christianity?

4. Peter fleshed out the meaning of "live such good lives among the pagans" (1 Peter 2:12) in 1 Peter 2:13–3:12. Study this section and write down some practical ways we can live to glorify God.

Chapter 10

Out of the Salt Shaker

What comes to your mind when you think of evangelism? Mission work? Mission work is evangelism, and we need committed people who will go out into foreign and domestic fields, taking the gospel where it is not well known. But congregations must not sit back and think that if they're sending missionaries, all their evangelistic responsibilities are fulfilled. You can't do evangelism by proxy.

Some think of the pulpit, the local evangelist. Many churches are like the department store that has its employees show up at the prescribed hour, lock the doors behind them, and spend eight hours selling goods to one another. No one from the outside is ever influenced. When we turn our assemblies into gospel meetings, we've missed what evangelism is about. The purpose of Sunday assemblies is to edify the church and praise God. We shouldn't try to do consistently in the building what ought to be done out in the world.

Some think of campaigns—going out and doing evangelism some place. Campaigns are an opportunity to grow spiritually, to see a bit of the world, to edify the church in an area in which it is weak and to publicize it in the community. Campaigns may be the only way the word can be broadcast where a congregation is weak, but it is not the model for ongoing evangelism, because everyone's talking to strangers, and strangers always have their defense systems up.

Finally, some think of evangelism as a sort of spiritual manhunt where someone announces that so and so is not a Christian and the God Squad mobilizes, forms a posse, and starts working on him. How would you like to be worked on?

For 2000 years, scripture has been pointing us toward a better plan for evangelism in the local congregation. We are to be a sweet smell that infiltrates our own community (2 Corinthians 2:15), a light that draws people from darkness (Matthew 5:14), salt that can be tasted (Matthew 5:13), an epistle that can be read (2 Corinthians 3:1-3).

Have you ever heard anybody say, "Poor me! I'm the only Christian in my office. I'm thinking about leaving my job to go into church work." What a strange attitude! The early church would have said, "Praise God, he's put me some place where no one else is a Christian, among people I can minister to!" You contact people on the job that you would never meet any place else. Haven't we said for a long time that there's no clergy-laity distinction, that we're all priests, all ministers? Then that secretarial job is church work. That factory job is church work.

You're involved in a place where God has put you. We are the salt of the earth. But what if all the salt stayed in the salt shaker? It doesn't do any good.

Some object, "The Bible says that bad company corrupts good morals, and here you are telling us to get out into the world, to mix with them and minister!"

I had just finished speaking at a North Carolina youth rally when the fellow after me used that verse to encourage teenagers not to have friends who were not Christians. An acquaintance of mine leaned over to me and whispered, "Jesus would have been in a lot of trouble, wouldn't he?" The point is well-taken. If this verse condemns building bridges with people who do not know Christ, then the Savior himself violated it, because he was always out there with people who needed him.

The verse occurs in the context of teaching about the resurrection (1 Corinthians 15). Paul wanted the Corinthians to consider the implications of the resurrection. If the dead generally are not raised, then Christ specifically could not have been raised. If Christ was not raised, then your hope is vain. If your hope is vain, you're the most pitiful people in the world, he concluded.

"If the dead are not raised, 'let us eat and drink, for tomorrow we die'" (1 Corinthians 15:32). If the dead will not be raised, then hedonism is the logical lifestyle. Bad thinking produces bad living. If you teach that there's no resurrection of the dead, it's going to influence the ethics of the church. "Bad company corrupts good character" (1 Corinthians 15:33). If you teach people that there's no resurrection, you'll see it fleshed out in bad living. In this context, the verse does not prohibit building bridges into the world.

Others appeal to the verse that says, "Abstain from all appearance of evil" (1 Thessalonians 5:22). Some have taken it to mean that we should stay away not only from evil but from everything that looks like evil to anyone else. You can see how it would cut down on ministry, however, if you could never be in a situation someone might interpret as shady. It would cut out a lot of the work of Jesus, for example.

But note other translations of the verse. The Revised Standard Version reads: "Abstain from every form of evil." The New International Version says, "Avoid every kind of evil." Not every appearance of evil, everything that might look evil, but every *form* of evil. Not, "Stay away from everything that somebody might raise an eyebrow about," but "Stay away from evil in all its forms."

The verse appears in the context of a study of prophecy. Some in Thessalonica could speak prophetic messages from God, but not all were impressed with their gift. They had probably heard some bogus prophecies and were suspicious of anything that was prophesied. So Paul said, "Don't put out the Spirit's fire. Don't ignore prophesies. But instead, test everything. Test the prophecies. Hold on to the good. Stay away from the evil." Some prophesying is legitimate. It comes from God. If it's good, hold on to it. If it's evil, get rid of it. Again, it doesn't keep us from ministry in the world.

Jesus spent his time in the world. He had friends who didn't have it all together spiritually. When he was criticized, he responded, "You people are just like kids sitting around saying, 'We played the flute and you didn't dance. We sang a dirge and you didn't mourn.'"

The life of John the Baptist was like a funeral dirge— ascetic, self-denying. He was the voice crying in the wilderness, "Prepare the way for the Lord!" A strange voice, but prophetic nonetheless. It was like a strong, mournful dirge. People said he had a demon.

On the other hand, Jesus had come playing the flute, calling people to this great, joyous festival of knowing God. He ate and drank with them. He was found among tax collectors and sinners. He even went home with one of them, a tax collector named Matthew. Why? "It's not the healthy who need a doctor but the sick .. .. , for I have not come to call the righteous but sinners" (Matthew 9:12-13).

When a doctor's beeper goes off, it tells us that a physician is needed because somebody's sick. It doesn't go off every time someone feels well. The physician is for those who are ill.

That's what Jesus was saying. "I'm here for those who are ill. The ones who think they have it all together spiritually I cannot minister to, so I am here for tax collectors and sinners—those broken souls who perceive a spiritual need." Aren't you thankful that he is!

Flavil Yeakley's book *Why Churches Grow* gives three models of Christian communicators in the world. The models are teacher, salesman, and friend.

The teacher model of communication could be called information transfer. One person tells other people what he knows. If you're not careful, it can sound like, "I know all the answers. I'm a walking dictionary to answer religious questions. Just ask me and I'll tell you." There are situations in which teachers need to give information. But out in the world with people who know a lot and have a lot of valuable experiences, it's not a good model.

The second model is that of the salesman. His basic method of communicating is manipulative monologue. Now, he may try to get some feedback, but he won't initiate genuine dialogue. He's just trying to manipulate you. He knows where he's going before he ever met you. He's got an agenda of what you need to hear, and he's going to work on you. He may try to elicit response, but just so he can get you where he wants you.

The third model is the friend. This approach centers on nonmanipulative dialogue, meeting people where they are. We want to exchange ideas. We want to grow together. If you've got something I need to know, I want that. I'm not trying to manipulate you just so I can tell you what I know. By the same token, I love you and want to share with you the things that have changed my life. Jesus was a teacher, but that wasn't his primary mode of relating to people. I don't know that he was ever a salesman trying to close a sale. He was a friend.

As Rebecca Pippert wrote in her book *Out of the Salt Shaker,*

> I am saying that by far the most effective, the most costly, and even perhaps the most biblical kind of evangelism is found in the person or groups who look at the people around them, those with whom their own life naturally intersects and then begin to cultivate friendships and to love them.

Some helpful principles for establishing relationships come from Jesus' time with people.

1. Do things together. In Matthew 9, Jesus was eating with Matthew, building a bridge by doing something together. We could do that, couldn't we? Most of us eat regularly. The people around us eat regularly. One way to establish a relationship is to do things together. We can expand the list to include racquetball, golf, tennis, gardening, woodworking, bridge, volunteer activities, quiltmaking, fishing, hunting, sewing, movies and concerts, service clubs, hiking, scouting, jogging, and so on.

2. Practice hospitality. Jesus couldn't invite people to his house, because for most of his life he had no place to lay his head. He was an itinerant preacher. But still he knew the comfort and sociableness of being in a home. So he went to Matthew's house, and suddenly the barriers were laid down at the door.

What did he say to Zacchaeus when he met him? "Zacchaeus, I'm going to your house today." He was always found eating with people, sitting in their homes, reclining at table, taking his shoes off. We can do the same.

3. Be available when people hurt. Jesus was a physician to the wounded. His heart went out to the lonely, the fearful, the prisoners, the suffering, the broken-hearted. In the same way, we can offer ourselves to those who hurt, starting with their felt needs and then going on to their ultimate needs.

God wants to use you wherever you are. You're in church work if you're in Jesus. You're a minister. You're a priest.

What kind of experience are people getting from your ministry? You may have one of two problems. You may be holy, but still in the salt shaker. If so, the challenge is to "Get out!" Or you may be out of the salt shaker but coming across more as garlic than as salt. If so, your life needs to be changed. Repent and let Jesus transform you to be his salt in the world.

Thought Questions for Chapter 10

1. Discuss the difference in the ministries of John the Baptist and Jesus. How was John like a dirge? How was Jesus like a flute player?
2. Evaluate the strengths and weaknesses you can imagine with the three communication models: teacher, salesman, friend.
3. The original recipients of 1 Peter knew what it's like to be "aliens" in this world. Those around them were ridiculing and maligning them. What insights can you

pick up from that letter for a church's evangelistic strategy?
4. How should the example of Jesus in relating to others affect our relationships?

Chapter 11

Audience Adaptation

Several years ago, Diane and I worshipped in a small congregation. Before we walked in, someone warned me to hide my Bible because it wasn't a King James Version. I tried to explain that it was my Greek Bible, but she said, "They think all those translations are liberal." So, I tucked my Greek Bible under my coat and went in.

The preacher covered every sin in the Bible plus a few extra. The main point, though, was mixed swimming. For about thirty minutes we heard a scathing attack of mixed swimming. The best I could tell, Diane and I were the only ones in the audience under the age of 80, and we were visitors. I had the feeling the message was a bit irrelevant, given the audience.

Several years ago, a missionary from Kenya spoke for chapel at Harding Graduate School. "Don't worship your ancestors," he warned us. "Don't worship your ancestors." I've never been tempted to do that. I honor those who have come before me, but ancestral worship is not one of my danger areas.

Then he paused and said, "You know, I'm not really speaking to you very well, am I?" We were all thinking, *No, not at all.* He said, "That's what I have to preach in Kenya. My message must begin with ancestral worship. If I'm ever going to reach out to those people I must begin where they are and then reach down into their ultimate needs. And yet, I wonder how many of you go out and preach on weekends speaking to people in irrelevant ways as well, talking about things they don't care about, speaking about items that don't concern them."

The point is well taken. If we're going to be the aroma of Christ in the world, we must be relevant. We must adapt to the listening audience.

One modern theologian said to "take the word and hurl it at them like a brick." Granted, there are times when we have to do just that—let the word speak for itself and cut through and penetrate to the dividing of bone and marrow. But if we do that consistently, we won't speak to very many people. Everybody will be ducking bricks, and the word will never penetrate.

We need an effective communication strategy for the gosepl as Christ invades culture. Let's consider some guidelines.

1. Adapt the message to the audience. "Are you talking about watering it down?" someone asks. No, not at all. You don't water down the message, you don't change it. You adapt it so people will hear it. That's the challenge to be not only faithful but contemporary, to have a first-century message with twentieth-century relevance.

Isn't that what Jesus did as he spoke to people? He preached to people who had heard it all before. They knew a million arguments for everything that could be said, just like a lot of people today who are raised in a religious environment. Once you announce the topic, their computer calls up that file and spits out on the screen exactly where the sermon is going. And off go the listening ears.

Jesus was speaking to people like that. They didn't

hear because they'd already heard it all. How do you preach to people who think they've got it all together?

Jesus used parables. He'd sneak around to the back door and catch them. The parable of the Good Samaritan is a prime example. The audience that first heard that was struck by the fact that it was a Samaritan who helped the injured man. That doesn't catch us any more, because we call it the parable of the Good Samaritan.

Paul wrote a great passage on audience adaptation (1 Corinthians 9:19-23). In it he said that he was open and flexible. When he preached to the Jews, he became Jewish. He went to the temple and offered a sacrifice, knowing that it didn't have redemptive value but dedicating it to the glory of God (Acts 21). When he was with Gentiles, he became like a Gentile. When he was with the weak, he was weak. The same would have been true, I suppose, when he was with the strong. Here's the reason: "I'm becoming all things to all men so that by all means I might save some of them" (1 Corinthians 9:22). Paul adapted to his audience.

There are several speeches of Paul's throughout Acts. Luke probably gave us a summary or the gist of them. It's interesting to note how the message differed with the audience. If all we're supposed to do is take Plan A and give it to everybody, Paul should have used the same methods wherever he went. But notice the variety. Paul wanted to be relevant in Antioch, in Lystra, in Athens. Everywhere he went, he adapted the message to the group.

Speaking in Antioch in Pisidia, basically to Jews, his message was geared toward his listeners:

Men of Israel and you Gentiles who worship God, listen to me! The God of the people of Israel chose our fathers and made the people prosper during their stay in Egypt. With mighty power he led them out of the country and endured their conduct forty years in the desert. He overthrew seven nations in Canaan and gave their land to his people as their inheritance. All this took about 450 years (Acts 13:16-19).

Then he told about Samuel, Saul, David, John, and Abraham before leading them to Christ. A Jewish audience could follow that line very well.

Later, in Athens, Paul saw the best that Greek philosophy and tradition could supply—the city of Socrates, Plato, and Aristotle. Speaking at the Areopagus, with the Acropolis, the Parthenon, and the statue of Apollo in view, he didn't just pull out the sermon outline from Antioch in Pisidia. He would have lost his audience completely. Instead he said: "Men of Athens! I see in every way you are very religious. I've seen all kinds of altars around—even one to an unknown God. Now the God that you're thinking about, I want to preach to you" (Acts 17:22, paraphrased). He then quoted a couple of their own prophets. One of them had said, "In him we live and move and have our being." And another said, "We are his offspring."

He didn't even start from the Old Testament. He started with their own thinkers. He adapted his message to meet the audience.

Who are you trying to reach? You've been thinking, I hope, about getting out into the world. How can you adapt the message of Christ to those about you? Where are they right now? You need to be wise in communicating the gospel. People are in different places in their lives.

2. Begin with felt needs. Everyone has a filter. You

have one. I have one. It strains out what I don't want to hear. It sifts through it all—what you say, what I hear on the radio, what I read in the newspaper—and allows me to ignore what I don't want to hear.

Many of the people around you don't care about the gospel. We've said for a long time, "Everybody's just waiting to hear the good news of Christ." That's not true. Studies show that about sixty per cent of non-Christians are very satisfied with life. They aren't just sitting around waiting for somebody to knock on their door. What they mean by happiness may be shallow, but we all interpret it in the light we have. So we need to work around their filters and begin with their needs.

That's what *Herald of Truth* and *Upreach Magazine* have done. A few have thought they compromised the gospel, but that's not it at all. They recognize that you have to begin with felt needs. If you talk about premillennialism, baptism, and church instruction, a lot of people will filter you out. But if you talk about the hurts of their families, their fears, anxieties, struggles, and tragedies, they'll let those filters down a bit. That's the principle of beginning with felt needs.

Abraham Maslow is not a good person to get your theology from, but he's got a good approach to felt needs. Maslow said we have different levels of needs, and you cannot address higher ones until the basic ones are met. In other words, if people are hungry, if their stomachs are growling for food, they won't care about your system of faith. First they need to eat, then maybe they'll listen.

It starts with physiological needs—clothing, food, water, shelter. The church must minister in those areas. Some might call that a social gospel. That's just a pejorative way to say "Don't do it!" But it was done in the Bible. It's good strategy, and you don't just do it to reach the top needs. You do it because it's right, because Jesus did.

Next you have safety and security needs. Some people feel isolated, unsure of themselves, in need of community, love, and affection. Should the gospel appeal to those needs? Certainly.

Then comes esteem, and finally, self-actualization, which for Christians would mean knowing your place at the cross of Christ.

The communication strategy begins with felt needs. Where are people right now, the people around you, on this scale? They won't want to know about ultimate needs until you've addressed the fundamentals. Are their families hurting? Then help them with the family. Do they need clothes? Then give them clothes.

Let's see how Jesus did it. He met a blind man (John 9). What did he do? He gave him sight. What did he do then? Did he preach the message to him? No, he left. He met the man where he was and then went on his way. That should tell us that we can give a cup of water in Jesus' name without sticking a gospel tract in it.

Another time he met a woman who had made the tiresome journey to Jacob's Well. Jesus said, "Can I have a drink?" It disturbed her that a man would speak to a woman, or that a Jew would speak to a Samaritan. Then Jesus said, "Would you like to know about living water?" It's a beautiful example of beginning where somebody is—meeting her immediate needs.

Is it manipulation? It can very well be. If I feed you in order to baptize you, I may be trying to manipulate you. If I'm always talking over here so I can get over there, I may be trying to manipulate you. Naturally, I want to do that, because my faith is important to me. But if everything is contingent on getting someplace else, it's manipulation.

Tom Peters' book **A Passion for Excellence** illustrates this fact. Peters was asked to review a book on listening, empathy, and face-to-face contact, which normally he's very positive toward. But he hated the book because the gist of it was that you listen only so you can get somewhere else. You sit down in face-to-face contact so that eventually you can do what you really want to do. Empathy is just a show to get someplace else. That's manipulation.

When I say begin with felt needs, I mean really be attuned to people. Meet them where they are. We say we're soul-winners. That's true. But we're more than that. We're people lovers. If I can relieve some anxiety, take care of somebody's kids and give him some relief, take a meal when somebody's had a death in the family, include her in some recreation that gives self-esteem— I'm beginning to communicate the gospel.

3. Seek eventually to meet ultimate needs. You have to begin where people are, and you don't manipulate them to get some other place. But because our faith is important to us, we pray that ultimately our relationships will lead others to become Christians. If they don't have that inclination, stay with them. Don't drop them. But eventually, we want to mention, "You know, when you get a moment, I'd like to discuss some spiritual issues that are important to me. I think you'll find them interesting.

Here are some things you need to talk over with them:

• The place of scripture. You don't have to iron out all the details. They don't need to know everything about scripture. But at least establish it as as good source of information about Christ.

• Who Jesus is. They need to know that he is what he claimed to be, both from God and from man. He comes from both worlds. He's deity and yet humanity.

111

• The concept of sin. It's not just some sledge hammer that fundamentalist pulpits use to drive somebody to guilt, but it's what's gone wrong with this world. It's responsible for the chaos, and each of us is caught up in it and is separated by it from the Creator. That's what's wrong with us.

• Grace. Grace is the answer to sin. You can't ever run away from sin. You can't earn your way out of it. You can only look heavenward and say with Paul, "By the grace of God, I am what I am."

• Faith. Man must reach up toward God, not ever able to earn grace, but thankfully accepting the free gift of salvation. An obedient faith comes to the point of baptism, where we enter into a relationship with him.

• The church. You need to talk about the church as a fellowship—a group that meets together, encourages each other, and bears one another's burdens.

• The cost of commitment. When I'm immersed into Christ, everything is new (Romans 6). I'm wanting to be his, to die to myself and live anew for others. That's ultimately where we hope our relationships will go.

Peace Child is a great book on communication strategy by Don Richardson, a missionary to the Sawi tribe in New Guinea in the 1960s. He tried telling the gospel story to the tribe, but when he got to the part about Judas, everybody cheered. Judas was the hero of the story, because in their tribe betraying a close friend was an admirable thing to do. The closer the friend was, the better. So when Judas betrayed his master, the tribe thought it was great. They wanted to worship Judas!

Richardson was dismayed. That was not the goal of the story. So he backed up and rethought the gospel message in terms of the tribe. They had a custom that when they were at war with another tribe and wanted peace for awhile, they would take a newborn baby from each tribe and exchange them. Those were the peace children. As long as they were alive, the pact of peace was intact.

So he went back to them with the gospel message, "Jesus is God's peace child. We were at war with God. We were separated from him, and now God has sent this peace child. He's the way God is establishing reconciliation with us today." With that the gospel was communicated and people came to Christ.

That is our task today as we go out into the world. How do you communicate a risen Christ? It's up to you. But you adapt your message to those you are trying to reach. You begin with their felt needs and try to lead eventually to their ultimate needs.

Thought Questions for Chapter 11

1. Our teaching tends to be deductive: we give our conclusions and apply them appropriately. But the parables of Jesus are more inductive: he involved his hearers by starting with lively examples leading to some "surprise" conclusions. How could we involve people more in our teaching?
2. Discuss the difference in Paul's sermons at Lystra (Acts 13) and Athens (Acts 17).
3. Of what significance is the human "filter" to the Christian communication process?
4. Summarize in one paragraph (in your own words) what the Christian message is that answers our ultimate needs.

Chapter 12

Freedom From Guilt

Do you ever feel as though the Christian message is irrelevant in our technological age? It isn't! The cross and resurrection of Jesus address the three most haunting problems of our age: guilt (a problem with the past), meaninglessness (a problem with the present), and hopelessness (a problem with the future). This chapter will look at Christ's message for guilty people, and the final chapter will focus on his solution for meaninglessness and hopelessness.

Guilt is something inside us that says, "You've blown it! You haven't done what you ought to do. You've fallen short. Something is out of sync. You're out of alignment. You're not what you ought to be." We call it conscience, and I believe God is the one who instilled it in us. Unless your conscience has been seared, something at some point in your life nags at you and reminds you that man has been separated from God. Your iniquities have come between you and the Creator, and you're out of fellowship with him. It's the forces of sin in your life that have pulled you from God. What can we do about it? How do you get rid of guilt?

The world might tell us to deny those guilt feelings. Many psychologists operate from a non-Christian perspective. They say, "Get rid of those repressions that come from religion and your parents. You don't need them. They're just garbage you've picked up along the way. There's nothing wrong with you. Whatever you want to do, do it. Whatever you feel, feel it. There are no absolutes in life. You're okay."

The problem is that your conscience tells you you're loathsome. Denial doesn't help a lot, because you still have the problem of the conscience. There's something still nagging you, saying that things aren't right. You've offended some universal standard. There's something out of alignment that you must deal with, so denial just doesn't work.

You could try concealment. Achan tried that. He'd ripped off some things at Jericho that he wasn't supposed to have. The Israelites lost the battle of Ai, and Achan tried to hide the things he'd stolen. It doesn't work. It's like a businessman trying to shuffle some papers or a student trying to hide his cheat sheet. David tried concealment after he'd slept with Bathsheba. She was pregnant. He tried to cover up the tracks and get rid of the doubts in people's minds, but it didn't work.

Denial won't work. Concealment won't work. And neither will working to atone for your sins. Some may think, *If I can work harder and do more and get on with business, I can get rid of this nagging guilt in the back of my mind. I'm going to read my Bible more. I'm going to pray more. I'm going to go on every campaign possible, attend every devotional, everything at the church building. I've got to do everything possible to try to get rid of the guilt.* But the emptiness remains as guilt only gives birth to more guilt.

Paul gave the only answer for guilt in his first letter to the Corinthians. He began, "For I am the least of the apostles and do not even deserve to be called an apostle, because I persecuted the church of God" (1 Corinthians 15:9).

Paul looked to the past and said, "I did some things wrong. I blew it! This beautiful, sanctified, church of God is the very church I was out to persecute!" Did he say it with self-condemnation? Did he say it with guilt? No.

You can live with a knowledge of the past—you must since you can't really erase the memories—without self-condemnation. How? Here's a two-pronged approach:

1. Accept Grace. "By the grace of God I am what I am" (1 Corinthians 15:10a). Too often we feel that we got ourselves into the mess, and we have to get ourselves out of it. If I dig the hole, I have to crawl out. But Paul said, "That's not the way it works. I persecuted the church, but it's by the grace of God that I am what I am now."

It's God's initiative, God's work. It's the gift of God. He reached down to you. That's where some of the big words in the Bible come into play—atonement, propitiation, expiation, reconciliation. That's what it's all about it.

You blow it just as Adam blew it, just as David and many others blew it. You're one of the many people who've messed up, and you're out of fellowship with God. There's no way you can get back to him. You can work and work and work, and you'll never get back, because you've already separated yourself. God didn't leave. You did. So you can work for the rest of your life and not get back to God.

God has to take the initiative, and he did. Isaiah said concerning the servant of God:

Surely he took up our infirmities and carried our sorrows, yet we considered him stricken by God, smitten by him, and afflicted. But he was pierced for our transgressions. He was crushed for our iniquities; the punishment that

116

brought us peace was upon him, and by his wounds we are healed. We all like sheep, have gone astray. Each of us has turned to his own way; and the Lord laid on him the iniquity of us all (Isaiah 53:4-6).

That's where the cross comes in. God sent his Son. He died on the cross, taking your burden, your guilt. Lay it all down, and you can be cleansed. The righteousness of Christ is credited to your life (Romans 4:22).

It's not by your becoming morally perfect; it's not by your own righteousness; it's by the righteousness of *Christ* that God says, "All right. By your faith when you come into Christ in baptism, I'm going to declare you righteous." Then you're at one with God, you're justified, and all your sins are washed away.

Paul didn't live a neurotic life. He claimed those things he preached. He said, "I am what I am by the grace of God." No self-grandeur. No illusions. Just "I'm okay. I don't have to condemn myself. I don't have to walk around with my nose in the dirt."

2. *Accept the life of grace.* "His grace to me was not without affect. No. I worked harder than all of them. Yet not I but the grace of God which was with me" (1 Corinthians 15:10b).

The legalistic approach to the law says you need to perform so you can be accepted. Grace says you are accepted, so you're free to perform. Those are two entirely different perspectives. Paul said, "I am what I am by grace. I've been accepted by God, and therefore I want to live the grace-filled life. I want to live right and stop doing wrong."

If you claim the promises of grace without determining to live in light of them, you'll have problems with guilt. As you get into Christian activities and start doing right, your emotions will eventually come around to your actual state. They will confirm in your mind what has objectively taken place—God has forgiven you.

You can live free from the past. You don't have to be neurotic. If you're in the Lord Jesus, you don't go in and out of relationship with God. Your sins are washed away. You can do something bad and not be a bad person. You can be guilty without being a guilty person.

"If you walk in the light as he is in the light, the blood of Christ keeps washing away your sins" (1 John 1:7, paraphrased). You're not in Christ at 10 o'clock and out of him at 10:30, back in him at 11, and out again at 11:30. You stay there. You may do something wrong, but you're still guiltless before God because you've been accepted.

Some of the most guilt-ridden, fearful people in the world are in our churches. You can't talk to them about freedom from the past because they haven't experienced it. They sing, "My sin—oh the bliss of this glorious thought—my sin, not in part but the whole, is nailed to the cross and I bear it no more." But many don't believe it. They've continued to nurture guilt.

I got a letter from a fellow who said, "I'm feeling suicidal. I'm ready to take my life, and I don't understand why. Why do I feel so guilty? Why do so many around me feel so guilty when we preach forgiveness?" That's a real problem for many of us.

There are two kinds of guilt. One is objective guilt, or theological guilt. When you've done something wrong before God, you're guilty whether you feel it or not. Some people's consciences are seared. They live horrendous lives without feeling guilty, but they are.

The other kind of guilt is subjective guilt—your feelings of guilt and self-condemnation. Sometimes they correspond to real guilt, and you can deal with them by confessing and releasing them. But other times we condemn ourselves when there is no objective guilt. Either we've not offended God, we've just offended some of our own standards, or we've offended him, confessed it, then held onto it.

Guiltaholics. You see them everywhere. They feel bad about themselves. They're depressed. They're very lonely. They're angry at everyone, and they hate God because he's the one who's made them feel that way so long. It's as if God were pointing a finger at their chests and saying, "Shape up or ship out," twenty-four hours a day.

That's a tough way to live. People like that meet you on the sidewalk and analyze for thirty minutes why you didn't look at them, smile, and say, "Hi!" They think it's because you hate them. Inferiority, depression, loneliness—it goes on and on.

In one of Bruce Narramore's books, he wrote about a woman he was counseling. He asked her to write ten sentences beginning, "I am. . . ." Here's the way she began: "I am a poor mother. I am a disappointment to my parents. I am overweight. I am unhappy. I am divorced." Narramore said, "Ma'am, I didn't ask you to name ten bad things about yourself. Name ten good things."

Here are the kind of things she listed: "I try to be a good mother. I try to keep a clean house. I try. . . ." What was she saying? "I try to but I don't." Those were just ten sneaky ways of condemning herself again.

Too many of us do the same. We worry about burning a trail to heaven or burning one out of hell until we're neurotic about it. We can't enjoy our religion. We don't believe there is no condemnation for those who are in Christ Jesus. We feed this condemnation to ourselves: "I can't do enough. I have all this guilt. I've got to be perfect. I've got to be right, and unless I am, God will not accept me."

Some have neurotically lived that way for decades. They've tried to treat the symptoms, but they haven't got at the root of it. They've never let go of the guilt. God let go of it, but they won't.

Where does this self-condemnation come from? Sometimes it comes from our religious background. Whether people told us so or not, we perceive our religion as saying that we must be exactly like God before we'll ever be accepted. We've got to be perfect. We've reversed the order of the New Testament that says, "You're accepted. Therefore, grow in maturity to be like Christ." We're legalistic sometimes. "I'm trying to earn my way toward God. I've got sins in my life, so God can't accept me."

Sometimes it comes from our parents. Please, parents, be easy on your children. If you make your daughter feel she can never do enough—date the right boys, make good enough grades, be nice enough, dress right, look good—what does she start thinking? *I'm just a rotten, terrible person.* She starts projecting that onto God. Just as she can't be good enough for Daddy and Mom, she assumes she can never be good enough for God.

Sometimes it comes because of real sin in the past that we won't let go. College students in particular, as they reflect on sexual experimentation in the past, may feel guilty for years. It can destroy their spiritual lives. They won't forgive themselves. They nurture the guilt and get more and more depressed. They hate people who enjoy their religion, and eventually they can't stand God.

We can't tell our culture about the good news if we're neurotic ourselves. We need to release that baggage that's weighed us down for years. Confess it, release it, and go on. There is no condemnation for those who are in Christ Jesus.

You'll have tension in your life as you keep moving toward maturity. There may be tension of guilt as you try to become more like Christ, but that's different from the guilt that says, "I am not right before God."

Bruce Narramore also told of counseling a minister's wife. She was suicidal because her husband loved everyone but her, she thought. He was out every day, every night, saving everybody in town but never loving her.

As he worked with her, Narramore built up her self-esteem. She and her husband were going away for a few days to Disneyland. They got a babysitter, and off they went. On the way, she had an overwhelming urge to jump out of the car and kill herself.

Later she explained that she didn't feel she deserved a break. She didn't deserve a day at Disneyland. All those feelings came back. *You're not right. You've blown it. You're out of fellowship with God. You've offended people. You weren't good enough for your parents. You're not good enough for God. You're not good enough for the church.*

It's counter-productive, to say the least, to hold feelings of self-condemnation that have no basis. Not all guilt feelings are wrong. Sometimes they're God's way of reaching us through our consciences. But if you're living with Christ, imperfect as you may be, you need to quit feeling self-condemnation. The world needs to hear about freedom from the past. *But you cannot preach what you've never experienced yourself.*

Let's look at two kings of Israel, Saul and David. Both were guilty of terrible things. Saul handled his guilt by turning in on himself with worldly sorrow and committing suicide. David handled his by turning to God and letting go. David was saved by grace through faith.

Judas and Paul were both guilty men. They did terrible things. They hurt people who were important to God. Judas turned in on himself with condemnation and worldly sorrow and killed himself. Paul in the city of Damascus heeded the words of Ananias, "Why do you wait? Get up and be baptized and wash away your sins, calling on the name of the Lord." That's the Paul who told us, "I've done some bad things, but I am what I am by the grace of God."

As Howard Carter was going into King Tut's burial chamber, he had to pass through four shrines. Each shrine had a little ditty taken from Egyptian theology. When he got to the fourth shrine, the words on it said, "I have seen yesterday, and therefore I know tomorrow."

Those are some of the saddest words that could ever be spoken. I know what I did yesterday, therefore I know tomorrow. There's no escape. There is condemnation.

I believe in change. I believe a person can choose to let God save him. A person can choose to hand over the garbage of guilt and be cleansed in the blood of Christ. As he works toward maturity, he'll struggle along the way, but he can be sure that there is no condemnation for those who are in Christ Jesus.

Thought Questions for Chapter 12

1. Terms like atonement, propitiation, and justification sound a bit ethereal to many non-Christians. How could you "translate" those concepts in explaining to someone the meaning of Jesus' death?
2. This chapter has emphasized the grace of God that

saves us. Does this grace offer a license for us to live any way we want? Study Titus 2:11-14 and Romans 6.

3. Many Christians who continue to be plagued by guilt had some bad programming in their homes. What kind of family environments might particularly cause a person later to struggle with guilt? (For supplemental reading, see *Healing for Damaged Emotions*, by David Seamands.)

4. Why do guilt, depression, low self-esteem, and loneliness often come as a "package deal"?

Chapter 13

An End To Trivial Pursuits

An Answer to Meaninglessness

I love the story of *The Old Man and the Sea* for a couple of reasons—because it centers on the Atlantic Ocean, for which I have a great love, and because I see Hemingway as a prophet of our age. He understood the implications of the beliefs that surround us. Many people hold those beliefs without knowing their implications. They live as if there were meaning when actually they're driven to the conclusion that there is no meaning in life.

Hemingway's story is a parable for modern man. The old man believed he would catch a blue marlin that would exceed all other fish ever caught. Every day he journeyed out in his beat-up old boat, looking for that one great marlin. Every day he failed.

Finally he latched onto that blue marlin of his dreams. He pulled it up next to the boat. He didn't have modern equipment to bring it into the boat, so he left it in the water and began dragging it back to the coast. As he neared the coastal waters, a shark attacked the marlin and tore it to shreds.

Hemingway told us that that's what life is about. You go out every day looking for something special. You may think you've found it, but in the moment of crisis, you find it was all an illusion. There is no purpose for your boat's going out. The end of Hemingway's life was consistent with his view. It was suicide.

That's where many people around us are. If they aren't grounded in reality, they're forced into meaninglessness.

A brilliant physicist named Stephen Weinberg has written a book, *The First Three Minutes—A Modern View of the Origin of the Universe.* In it he said:

> It is almost irresistible for humans to believe that we have some special relation to the universe, that human life is not just a more-or-less farcical outcome of a chain of accidents reaching back to the first three minutes, but that we were somehow built in from the beginning.

He went on to say that that's all a myth, though, that we're just a purposeless outcome stemming from accidental origins.

> It is very hard to realize that this . . . is . . . an overwhelmingly hostile universe. . . . It is even harder to realize that this present universe has evolved from an unspeakable, unfamiliar early condition, and faces a future extinction of endless cold or intolerable heat. The more the universe seems comprehensible, the more it also seems pointless.

He's honest in saying that. Beginning where he is, he has to conclude that life is meaningless. There's no reason to go through the day, certainly through the years of a lifetime. It's all vanity.

Tom Peters, in the first of his two books on excellence, *In Search of Excellence,* quoted a psychologist named Ernest Becker who said, "Society . . . is a vehicle for earthly heroism. . . . Man transcends death by finding meaning for his life. . . . It is the burning desire for the creature to count. . . . What man really fears is not so much extinction, but extinction with insignificance."

Peters then described a psychological study in which a group of people were given a task, a bunch of puzzles to solve. There were a lot of distractions—people speaking Spanish and Armenian, people typing and running calculators, street noise.

The group was divided—half the people were given a button they could push if they wanted to stop the noise, while the other half had to grit their teeth and put up with it. Which group performed better on the test?

The people who had the button they could push did five times as well as the others. And they never once pushed the button! In other words, people could ignore the distractions *if* they had the knowledge that they could do something about them. On the other hand, knowing we have no control over our lives drives many people to despair.

There are two major problems with people in our society:

1. They're looking for meaning in the wrong place. They haven't found the right door, the place where meaning can be found. The book of Ecclesiastes begins, "I've run the gamut of life. I've seen everything there is to see, and it's all vanity." That's meaninglessness— bleak but honest.

Some, as they search for meaning, try possessions. "If I could just have 'X,' I could be happy." Maybe "X" is a condo at the beach. So they buy a condo, but there's no meaning there. Well, maybe "X" is a half-million-dollar sailboat. So they run out and buy it, and alas, all is vanity.

Others try systems of government. Elton Trueblood has said that Hitler's success was in calling the German youth to believe they were actors in a cosmic drama. Classic liberalism had shaken their faith. They were ripe for someone to say, "You can be actors in this cosmic drama, this faith, this system of government." That's how he enlivened a whole nation.

How do you account for Jonestown? Hundreds of people traipsed off to South America and committed suicide, following the voice of some egomaniac. He offered meaning.

Others knock at the door of sensuality—the Animal House approach to life. If they can live it up and throw off all restraints, surely there will be meaning for life. They live this Animal House life, which is really just an animal life, but there's no meaning.

Maybe it's position—being known. Can you recall people who bragged about the famous people they knew? Maybe they saw them in an airport one time. But that's their claim to fame.

At some point in life, I hope, we'll peel away the externals. There are moments of refining fire in people's lives when they decide, *I've got to start peeling away and see if there really is something that energizes me and drives me through life.*

At least twice in a person's life he's likely to face those issues: when he gets out of high school and at middle age. Some won't bother to ask as they leave high school. They'll take a class because you've got to take it to graduate, and they want to graduate because you've got to graduate to get a job, and they want a job because you've got to have a job to live. They don't know any other reason why they do it.

Others are more discerning. They start trying to relate everything in life to one system of meaning. "I'm taking this class because of this meaning in my life. I want a job because I want to enhance this aspect of my life." College is a time when those questions need to be asked.

At middle age, people realize they've probably hit their peak. Their plans have either been realized or not. Life may seem futile. That's when you see men and women racing around town doing things they haven't done in twenty years. They're trying to relive their youth because they found they were onions: they kept peeling and nothing was left.

2. They're waiting for meaning to show up. Have you ever heard somebody say, "I'm looking for myself"? Whether they know it or not, they're accepting a philosophical tradition that goes back to Plato and that says your pre-existent self is waiting to be discovered. But there is no pre-existent self. Your self is waiting to be created by committing yourself to something that's grounded in reality.

Meaning for Today

The New Testament speaks of the new life, new creation, new being. It's a being you create by the Spirit of God. You commit yourself to something real, and there's a new self. You're not just waiting for some Monday morning when yourself shows up. You won't like it if it does! You're taking the initiative and committing yourself to something that provides newness.

Jesus wasn't looking for himself. He knew who he was. He made a grandiose claim: "I have come down from heaven not to do my will but to do the will of him who sent me" (John 6:38).

Jesus never lacked purpose. He came bearing life— new, significant life. That's what he brought from the Father. He didn't have a lot of loose ends. They were all

128

tied together by the thing that drove him through life—doing the will of the Father.

We can see it when he was thrown into a garden and came face to face with his imminent crucifixion. He struggled, but ultimately he said, "Not my will but thine be done." He was committed to that meaning for his life. When they put him on a cross, he forgave those who persecuted him, contrary to all human inclinations, because he wanted to do the will of the Father. Even in the moment of death, he said, "Into your hands I commit my spirit."

I want to be able to live that way. I don't want to have everything segmented in my life. I want it all united so I can say, "This is what life is about. That's what I'm trying to do with my family, my life, my church, my job. This is where it all unifies." Jesus could say that.

"I tell you the truth, unless you eat the flesh of the Son of Man and drink his blood, you have no life in you" (John 6:53). Unless you participate in Jesus' life and start doing the will of the Father, you won't find it either.

The apostle Paul wrote his young friend Timothy to call him back to the faith. Timothy was too timid in suffering, so Paul used himself as an example (2 Timothy 1:8-12).

What a beautiful way to end your life, as Paul was about to do! He wrote, "Timothy, I want you to think with me. I've committed my life to this reality. I'm grounded in the truth that God sent his Son who died on the cross, who was raised again, and because I know whom I believe, I'm committed to him." Then he concluded, "For I am already being poured out as a drink offering, and the time has come for my departure. I have fought the good fight, I have finished the race, I have kept the faith" (2 Timothy 4:6).

That's not to say that Paul had done everything he could have done. He probably could have baptized more people. He could have started more churches. He could have fed more who were hungry. He hadn't done everything he'd like to have done, but he'd done the one thing he wanted to do above all others—he'd glorified God and done his will.

An Answer to Hopelessness

Ernest Hemingway's life ended in suicide. He had a brilliant mind, a great evangelical heritage, and a wonderful pen, but they were not tied together with anything transcendent. Paul, on the other hand, had meaning for his present life and a glorious hope for the future. He described that hope in his letter to the church at Rome (Romans 8:18-25).

We need to understand two terms in coming to grips with the hope Paul expressed: suffering and salvation. Hope lives in tension between the two. Suffering says the world's in trouble. It's groaning in pain, subjected to frustration. Salvation says we already partake of that which God has given us though we've yet to experience the fulness of it. We have the firstfruits of the indwelling Spirit of God, but we haven't realized the fulness of salvation, so we have a foot in both worlds.

Many in our culture don't have this tension of living between the worlds. Some ignore the suffering part. They have taken a large shot of the adrenalin of positive humanism. Man has no limits, they believe. He can get out. He can grow. He can be anything he wants if you just educate him enough.

Or maybe they've had it with suffering, so they've decided to ignore it. They shrug their shoulders. They don't care anymore. It's behind them. They don't want to talk about pain. They'll just ignore it and pretend it isn't there.

More people see the suffering but have no concept of salvation. If you believe that all that exists is what is here and now, you are left with a big, fat zero. Nothing.

You might try to claim there's something, but if you're living only in the world of suffering without some concept of salvation, there's no hope. When all your trivial pursuits and all your excellence come to their conclusion, all is destruction. The only thing you can talk about with credibility is nuclear annihilation. It tears into the guts of the world.

Some worry about having a relevant message, but if you know the hurts of society, if you know the utter hopelessness, you won't be irrelevant. You need to drive people to their logical conclusions. What are you doing with your life? Then what are you going to do? Then what? Then what? Finally, they have to address the grave.

There's no answer for the grave outside of the kind of hope Paul wrote about. The sting of death is too sharp. It's too poisonous. No wonder so many in our society take Valium as though it were Flintstone vitamins or snorkle down booze as if grain were going out of existence or snort cocaine as if it were a gift from heaven. These are the anesthesia that prevents them from thinking about how dead the grave really is.

One of the saddest plays ever written is Samuel Beckett's **"Waiting for Godot."** Two men are waiting for this character named Godot to come along. Their lives are pitiful. But somebody's told them that, if they'll just wait until Godot comes along, everything will come together. All the pieces of the puzzle will fit. So they sit around waiting for Godot. He's the embodiment, the harbinger of hope.

The tragedy of the play is that there's no Godot. He's a myth. Beckett's point wasn't so much about Godot as about God.

The Bible tells of two other men who had been waiting. They'd had a dream, but the grave had stripped it from them. They'd placed their hope in something they thought could surpass the grave. "We had hoped that he was going to be the one to redeem Israel," they said (Luke 24).

Pseudo-messiahs cannot surpass the grave. Education can't, as promising as it seems. Modern science can't. It has no significant answer to that kind of question. You won't get it from money and financial pursuits, either. None of the things culture is enamored of can surpass the grave.

The sting of death is great, but we have the answer. It's the answer Paul gave. The new procurator Festus had inherited a problem, and Paul was it. The Jews wanted to hang him, but Festus's predecessor could find no law he'd broken. So he just left him in limbo until somebody else could deal with him.

As Festus took office, Paul came before him and said, "You have no right to judge me. I appeal to Caesar." Now Festus had to come up with a charge to explain why Paul was being sent to Nero. The best he could come up with was that Paul bucked the customs of the Jews, and that wasn't good enough.

Fortunately, King Agrippa showed up. He was king over an insignificant kingdom to the north, but at least he knew something about the Jews. Paul was brought before him, and Paul raised a series of questions.

1. "Why should any of you consider it incredible that God raises the dead?" Paul started by allowing the supernatural. If there's a God, it's entirely possible that he raised somebody from the dead. Science proves it's not possible? No. Science only deals in things that occur repeatedly, so you can test them. The resurrection was not a recurring event. Science can't deal with that.

2. *"King Agrippa, do you believe the prophets? I know you do."* "Agrippa, you believe something about the Bible," Paul was saying. "You know the prophets. Don't you know that the Old Testament is incomplete? There's this sense of yearning, of pieces of a puzzle that are not put together yet. It's like the first act of a play; you keep waiting for the curtain to rise again."

Paul was saying from scripture that if you have any kind of confidence in what the Old Testament prophets were saying, it's logical that Jesus was the Christ, because he's what they said would come.

3. *"Agrippa, you've lived in this land a long time. Don't you know it wasn't done in a corner?"* There's a song that's popular today: "You ask me how I know he lives. He lives within my heart." That's part of it. You should tell people what you know from your own experience. But that's only half of it. The other half is the empty grave.

That's where culture has stumbled all along. The grave. How are you going to deal with it? How do you explain the early Christian church if not for the empty grave? How do you explain the radical change in some of the early disciples? How do you explain the growth of the early church?

"It was not done in a corner." If they wanted to investigate, it was just a short walk to the tomb. If there was any question about whether the grave was full or empty, all they had to do was look. It's the explanation of the church's very existence and you cannot explain it without the resurrection.

The hope of the resurrection is truly a message of good

news to a culture strangled by suffering. A new light begins to dawn.

An experiment was conducted at the University of North Carolina with two rats. One was put in a jar half-filled with water. A lid was placed on top so it appeared that there was no escape. That rat drowned in three minutes. The other was put in a jar also half-filled, but with a space at the top that was not closed. That rat swam for thirty-six hours before drowning. The difference was hope, and people are much the same.

We can do amazing things if we have hope. It becomes a solid anchor amid hurricane-force winds (Hebrews 6:19). That hope is real—as real as the resurrection of Jesus. What a relevant, timely message we have when we're asked about the hope that's within us!

Thought Questions for Chapter 13

1. Ernest Hemingway once wrote: "I live in a vacuum that is as lonely as a radio tube when the batteries are dead and there is no current to plug into." In what sense is that a statement for our age?
2. Study Romans 8:18-21. How does hope relate to suffering and salvation there?
3. Some harsh realities must be faced if Jesus wasn't raised from the dead. What are those realities that Paul discussed in 1 Corinthians 15:12-19?
4. Suicide continues to steal the lives of many people. How do the high rate of suicide and the problems discussed in this chapter relate?